People
Profit

PEOPLE PROFIT
How to Improve Your Bottom Line by Investing in Those Above It
Copyright © 2025 Sandra Coker

ISBN: 978-1-964046-59-4

This publication is designed to provide accurate and authoritative information regarding the subject matter contained within. It should be understood that the author and publisher are not engaged in rendering legal, accounting, or other financial services through this medium. The author and publisher shall not be liable for your misuse of this material and shall have neither liability nor responsibility to anyone with respect to any loss or damage caused, or alleged to be caused, directly or indirectly by the information contained in this book. The author and/or publisher do not guarantee that anyone following these strategies, suggestions, tips, ideas, or techniques will become successful. If legal advice or other expert assistance is required, the services of a competent professional should be sought. All rights reserved. No portion of this book may be reproduced mechanically, electronically, or by any other means, including photocopying, without the written permission of the author. It is illegal to copy the book, post it to a website, or distribute it by any other means without permission from the author.

Expert Press
11610 Pleasant Ridge Rd.
Suite 103, #189
Little Rock AR 72223
www.ExpertPress.net

Editing by Tamma Ford
Copyediting by Hannah Skaggs
Proofreading by Abby Kendall
Text design and composition by Emily Fritz
Cover design by Casey Fritz

People Profit

How to Improve Your Bottom Line
by Investing in Those Above It

Sandra Coker

This book is dedicated to my amazing mother.

She is my greatest cheerleader, my inspiration, and my unwavering supporter.

Her belief in me has been the foundation of my success. Her encouragement has carried me through every challenge and setback I have ever had. She always reminds me to follow my dreams and that I am capable of more than I ever imagined. This book—and every endeavor I pursue—is a reflection of her love, strength, and guidance throughout my life and career.

This is for you, Mom. I love you.

Contents

	Introduction	**1**
1	**What You Don't Know About Service**	**7**
	Internal Customers	8
	The Pain Bleeds Outward	10
	Transactional vs. Relational	12
	The Problem with Service	15
	People Profit	22
2	**Get Your (Internal) House in Order**	**25**
	Engagement Surveys	26
	The Psychological Contract	26
	And Speaking of Costs	29
	Happy, Engaged Employees	30
	Disgruntled Employees	34
	Those Reviews	37
	People Profit	39
3	**Employees Are Your Biggest Asset**	**41**
	Is There a Career Path?	42
	Make Recruitment and Retention Easier	45
	Not a Farm: No Silos	47
	What Is This "Valuing" Thing?	52
	The Cost of Turnover	55
	People Profit	56
4	**Choosing the Right Manager**	**59**
	Leaders	60
	Managers	61
	Choosing for EQ	63
	Promoting the Right One	65
	Finding the Unlikely Leader	66
	Create Energy	67
	People Profit	71

5	**Leadership Styles**	**75**
	The Transactional Leader: The Taskmaster	76
	The Autocratic Leader: The Decider	76
	The Consensus Leader: The Collaborator	77
	A Tale of Two Leaders #1	78
	The Transformational Leader: The Visionary	80
	What's Your Leadership Game?	81
	How to Level Up Your Leadership Style	83
	The Role of Standards in Leadership	87
	Portrait of a Bad Leader	90
	A Tale of Two Leaders #2	91
	People Profit	94
6	**Your External Customer and Your Market Reputation**	**95**
	Customer Personas	96
	Your Reputation in the Market	102
	Market Reputation: The Silent Salesperson	105
	Marketing and Branding	107
	People Profit	115
7	**Mistakes, Recovery, and Leveling Up**	**117**
	Mistakes Are Inevitable	118
	Turning Mistakes into Growth Opportunities	120
	Just Solutions	123
	Celebrating Success	126
	People Profit	130
8	**Be the Disruptor in Your Field**	**133**
	What Exactly Is a Disruptor?	135
	Internal Customer Disruption	138
	External Customer Disruption	144
	All for the Wow	145
	People Profit	152
Conclusion		**155**
	The Heart of Your Business	156
About the Author		**159**

Introduction

This book was born from noticing a recurring issue in the world of business, service, and customer satisfaction. In various environments, from restaurants and retail businesses (whatever the product) to service calls—it often felt like genuine care for customer needs was missing.

This led to a deeper question: How much of this gap stems from a company's internal culture? When employees aren't supported or empowered, their ability to connect with customers often suffers.

This book delves into how a company's internal environment profoundly shapes the experiences it delivers to clients. As an entrepreneur, business owner, and someone passionate about people, I've noticed a growing gap between the level of customer service businesses provide and the expectations clients bring to each interaction. This isn't just about individual experiences; it has a ripple effect on a business's ability to achieve predictable, sustainable growth.

Spending time out in the world—whether with friends, family, or client companies—I see many businesses struggling to thrive, and it's often linked to this disconnect in service. Owners and managers may not fully see how this impacts their goals for growth and profitability.

Why read this book? It introduces a perspective on customer service that may reveal that overlooked population called *"internal customers"* essential to every business.

This book explores customer service from a different angle—one that may challenge conventional ideas. I present a view of customer service that goes beyond the usual definitions, reshaping how we think about service in any setting.

Serving others in a way that creates an authentic, repeatable (and repeated) experience will influence your business as well as your life in profound ways. When we stop simply going through the motions—smiling or saying the right things with no feeling behind them—and instead start genuinely connecting with clients, listening to them, and responding to their needs in more relevant ways, we begin to create a positively memorable experience for them.

With over thirty years of experience in management, business ownership, and customer care, I've come to appreciate how meaningful client interactions create a lasting impact. I've come to understand the power of delivering a "wow" experience. This book is here to inspire a fresh approach to service, encouraging thoughtful connections with others in every interaction.

Consider these few questions to help frame your understanding of client service:

- Have you ever walked into a restaurant, stood at the hostess station, and been ignored by servers walking by?

- After ordering a product online and receiving something completely different, have you ever been unable to find customer service contact information on the seller's website to get a refund or a return label?

- Have you ever waited in a retail line that is ten people deep, with only one register open, while staff members mill around without acknowledging the line or providing help?

- Have you ever gone into a big-box hardware store and wandered aimlessly without being offered assistance?

- Have you ever needed to call a service provider for a household emergency and gotten only their voicemail—even though they boast a 24/7 service?

- Have you ever stood at a bar, trying to get a bartender's attention, only to be ignored as you wait endlessly?

These mundane but frustrating scenarios are common and contribute to the poor reputation of the customer service industry. It's said that the United States is a service economy, but we have become less and less focused on service. While it's true that people in many industries are paid at minimum or near-minimum rates, that doesn't excuse poor service by the employee or the business. When someone accepts a job, they commit to upholding the company's values and standards of service.

My messages are for business owners and executives who have let their own standards slip by not reiterating them in every orientation and onboarding, every training session, every meeting, and every innovative action they take. Having your employees embrace the culture of your company is key to success. However, you can't expect them to live your culture if you and your team haven't defined it clearly yourselves. That's an entirely separate topic for another discussion but knowing your company's culture is crucial.

Let me share a personal story to illustrate my point.

As I was in the process of writing this book, I was about to get married for the second time. I had been divorced for eight years and had faced quite a bit of adversity during that time, so this wedding held deep meaning for me. I was excited about every aspect of it. We'd found a beautiful venue on Cape Cod, where I grew up. My eighty-one-year-old mother found a lovely golf course with a restaurant and event space that had just reopened for events after the COVID-19 pandemic. We secured the exact date we wanted in September—one of the most beautiful months on Cape Cod. I felt like it was meant to be.

None of us had tried the food at the venue, so we decided to have dinner there on Mother's Day to celebrate and test it out. I called a month in advance to make a reservation for ten people—my family and my fiancé—and was told we didn't need one. A couple of days before Mother's Day, I called again to confirm, and again they said not to worry and to arrive thirty minutes before we wanted to eat.

Despite my hesitation about their casual approach to large parties (based on my hospitality experience), my fiancé and I arrived early to ensure everything was in order. To my surprise, when we arrived, we were greeted with "We're done serving for today." Shocked, I asked for clarification only to be told again that they were finished serving. I explained that I had called twice and informed them that we had ten people, including my elderly mother, coming for Mother's Day dinner. The hostess, a young woman, simply repeated the same line—no empathy, no apology, and no reasons given.

Frustrated, I asked to speak to the manager, who also told me they were done serving for the day, without any hint of remorse. Only when I mentioned that I was getting married at their venue in a couple of months did she finally explain *why* they were closed for the day—a pipe had burst, and they had no water!

Had the hostess been trained to offer a "So sorry" and been allowed to explain their very understandable reason for closing, I might have reacted differently. Instead, I had to fight to get an explanation, which left a bitter taste. If it hadn't been so close to our date, I would have found another location.

Stories like this one highlight the critical role of our response in defining the experience of our clients and customers and, in turn, the reputation of the business. It's not about that client, diner, patient, buyer, or online purchaser—at least not at first. It's about another type of customer entirely. Turn the page, and I'll explain.

Chapter 1

What You Don't Know About Service

Many people in the business world think service is just about their clients or customers. The idea is to provide "customer service" to the people or businesses buying your products or services. For many businesses, service is only about how your frontline staff smile, dress, and greet customers face-to-face or over the phone, and how you present to your buying public.

Service is not only about that. Far from it. That's a mere start.

Service is a much more holistic concept, and for our purposes here in these pages, I'd like you to expand your thinking about service in two ways:

1. Bring the idea of service internally, inside the business, and look at your internal customers. What is your internal customer service like?

2. Then take service externally and look at your buying, paying customers. What is your external customer service like?

Internal Customers

Your internal customers are your team members, your staff, your employees—every single individual working in your business.

Note that I'll be variously calling them your internal customers, your staff, your team, or your employees. They are your company's entire internal network of people who make it all happen, wherever in your business they are employed.

Internal customer service is where most businesses miss the boat. This is where—when pressed—executives, leaders, managers, and supervisors can't really say they know what we're talking about.

Talking to leaders for the first time about their internal customer service produces a predictable effect. Their reaction—across industries, company sizes, ownership, and history—is that cross-eyed look that shouts, "What do you mean, *internal customer service?*"

I meet clients who are losing market share. They're losing customers and revenue. They're getting bad reviews on all the review sites and social media. Their customers and clients are not out there shouting from the rooftops how great their business is, promoting them, sending them referral business, or leaving great reviews. And worse, they are bleeding staff—turnover is sky-high.

The first reflex of those clients is to fix their customer service processes—to give all their attention to *external* customers who are panning them and running for their competition. However, to really get things right, their first action should be to look for an *internal customer service* problem and fix that.

This is not just about updating your processes and procedures to be more efficient. That's mere mechanics (though many businesses don't pay nearly enough attention to that, either). Internal customer service is also how you treat everybody you work with.

As leaders and as an organization and culture, take a look at your peers, your coworkers, and people in the various departments differently. They're inside your business, so think of them from now on as your internal customers. At best, the thoughtful, attentive way you treat external customers is the way to treat internal customers.

Internally, familiarity can lead to a sense of comfort with colleagues after working together for so long. Professional boundaries and communication standards that would be applied to external customers may begin to fade, replaced by a too-familiar tone—sometimes letting expressions of frustration, sarcasm, or condescension slide in your communication with each other without a second thought.

Let me say this: Your internal customers have some thoughts about that treatment and that way of addressing each other. Those behaviors, attitudes, and reactions happen in the family atmosphere, but it shouldn't be that way in the workplace. Workers are not family. They're people who are working together toward the same set of goals in a business. There should be some synergy. They're a team.

The Pain Bleeds Outward

Here's the cause-and-effect that most businesses fail to identify. If the internal customers—the organization's teams—are going through some dysfunction, your external customers will feel that pain. If the dysfunction lasts and lasts without correction or improvement, your external customers will start looking for alternatives to get their products or services. Your competitors are waiting.

Serving internal customers with the same attention as your external customers can only benefit from the external customer's experience with your business. This internal customer service approach has a ripple effect that supports improvements in top-line sales revenues and bottom-line profits as I will be demonstrating in later sections.

It doesn't matter whether you are a manufacturing plant, hospitality business, retail store of whatever size, bargaining unit business, nonprofit corporation, or professional services firm. When the workflow isn't smooth, there are hiccups in communication, or someone isn't pulling their weight—anytime the operation needs to stop to fix something—that's an external customer service problem in the making. Fixing those internal customer service problems must become a priority. Fixing them immediately prevents a disastrous ripple effect from reaching your external clients.

If there's redundancy in paperwork, your people get frustrated. If there are contradictory ways to do a task or no process provided to do it, that's frustrating to your internal customers. If your managers are in put-out-the-fire mode, internally there is turmoil. Sooner or later (but probably sooner), your external customers are going to feel the pain. So will your business, at both the top and bottom lines of your profit and loss statement.

When external customers feel that nothing's getting done for them, for example, when they are not getting their deliveries on time or just not getting the service they expect, they will not care one bit why or what your challenges are. They only know they want what they want from your business and aren't getting it. Again, your competitors are waiting.

If you take care of your internal customers, your external customers will be fine. Focusing solely on external customer interactions while expecting internal teams to simply 'be nice to each other' may limit the potential for greater success. Investing in a range of internal customer services can be a key driver for meaningful improvements in business growth and bottom-line performance. Bottom-line results start with internal customers, not external ones.

Transactional vs. Relational

Often with client care and customer service, we think about two things. We think first about the transaction. When you go to a bank teller, most of the time it's transactional. The bank employee facing you is trained to take your deposit or give you the cash you want to withdraw, then a receipt. If that transaction goes smoothly, great.

It's a transaction, sure, but it's more. The "more" is the relationship. That's why everyone who is forward-facing should be trained in how to be relational as well as how to perform the transaction as expected.

Yes, we are transacting with our clients. Yes, we are trading goods or services for money, and yes, it can be sort of cut-and-dried in the transactional sense. But the relationship is what helps us create loyalty and an ongoing relationship with customers—a.k.a. repeat and referral business. There are plenty of full-service banks out there. All things being equal transaction-wise, loyalty comes from the relationship a customer has with that bank's people.

It's the relationship—the human interaction piece—that brings a buyer or client back to you for a second time or more. It's the lack of that piece that sends them scooting to your competition.

Relationships get them feeling confident and refer others to your company for the goods and services you provide. Training that emphasizes only tactics and transactions may leave an essential part of skill development unaddressed—namely, human interaction, conversation, and communication—relationship-building skills. In a transactional business, when interactions remain purely transactional, fostering client loyalty can be challenging.

Let me expand on my bank example. When I was opening my first business, I had a relationship with a banker who believed in what I was trying to do. I had never owned a business before, but because he knew me and he knew what I was all about, his bank took a risk on me. Because of our relationship, I was able to start the business and owned it for seven years. I was debt-free by year three. I saw my banker every time I was in the bank, would have a brief chat, would feel connected.

Twelve years later, when I opened my second business, my original banker had moved on, and his successor at the bank had no established connection with me. What became clear was that he didn't want one! The new banker didn't follow up, check in, or make any effort to build a relationship. Meanwhile, at another bank, someone else did. That's where I took my business. I gave my business to the second bank because I had a better relationship with the interfacing person at that bank.

All things being equal, it's all about relationships and it's really important to examine relationships in light of your internal customers, too.

We want to be sure that the service we offer our external customers is genuine and meaningful—authentic, relevant, and natural rather than forced or fake. No one gets that kind of service from a staff that is pulled every which way by their leaders, isn't properly hired or trained for the tasks involved, and doesn't perceive leadership as seeing the value of what they do on the company's behalf.

As we're performing a transactional set of tasks for others, we're asking questions and connecting to be sure we're creating an atmosphere that quietly communicates, "You can trust my business internally and externally. I'm going to do what you need me to do for you. I'm going to perform the task for you, but I'm also going to care about why I'm performing this task for you. I'll talk to you as a valued partner to our business."

When my team and I go into manufacturing plants where no external customer ever enters, this is just as true as it is with buyer-facing internal staff. It's true for all businesses. We worked with a client that manufactures parts for prosthetic knee replacements. It's a machine shop. It's sweaty work. They have three shifts of workers who come in and grind parts all day. They use computer-aided design and operate various types of machinery.

When we were hired, there was some conflict in the organization. We started working with the leaders and the floor foreman, talking with them about what internal customer service was. We started to talk about giving their employees meaning, and it was like Greek to them. They had never heard anything like this before. To the credit of the foreman and other leaders, they heard us out.

We did our best to express this in a way they could grasp: "As you're educating your production teams on what they're doing, you need to remind them that a real person will be using what they manufacture to increase their comfort in life." That got us some nods of understanding.

"Remind them that the part they're producing could end up in the body of someone they love. It could be their grandmother, their mom, or themselves." That's when the leaders' and foremen's eyes opened wide. They got it!

"When you're training your frontline workers in service, inform them that it's about the end user. These are not just random parts for another machine. Understanding this makes what they do relevant, important, and meaningful. It can motivate them to perform their tasks at a much higher level." No one had ever framed labor jobs like this before, but when they started doing it, production quality and other metrics improved.

The Problem with Service

For the most part, the word *service* is overused. It has brought us to a place where no one understands what service is, should be, or could be, or why we should bother.

When you ask almost anyone in business, "What's your differentiator? How are you unique?" they say it's their service. You hear that constantly. If you probe to find out what they mean by service and to describe theirs, suddenly they run out of words.

What *does* service to your customer mean? The immediate answer should be something like this:

- It's a focus on relationships; we know them better than anyone.

- We understand what our clients expect from us.

- We get to know them, so we're proactive in helping them achieve their goals.

- We get to know them well so we can anticipate their problems and provide a solution before they ask for one.

This is what a great relationship-based service allows you to say with certainty: "We develop a personal relationship so that even if they decide to leave us, they leave with a good taste in their mouths. We know that if they leave us, it's for money reasons or for some other reason they're willing to tell us. If they go somewhere else and don't get the relationship they have with us, we're confident they will come back to us because they know we have a strong understanding of their needs, goals, and wants and the changes they're undergoing."

That's why my team consistently guides our clients to emphasize, not just "our service," but rather "our relationships" and the collaborative work we're doing as partners for each other.

Through our work with a diverse range of businesses, we've found that a transactional-plus-relational approach—going beyond transactional service alone—applies effectively across various industries. It not only applies, but it also works to change everything about your business, including the bottom line.

When I bought my fitness center in 2008, I aimed to apply a blend of transactional and relational approaches to running and growing the business. With limited funds beyond a bank loan, I had planned strategies around the three hundred members who were promised in the purchase agreement. But on day one, I discovered only eighty-eight members were actively paying. The previous owners had presold one-year memberships, inflating the numbers. Suddenly, I faced a much larger challenge than expected. Determined to succeed, I committed to providing an exceptional experience for those eighty-eight members, believing that building strong connections with them could help grow the business sustainably. With competition from a new big-box gym down the street, we set out to create a different kind of fitness experience where members were more than just a number, more than just a subscription fee. A big part of that focus was on building a dedicated, customer-centered team. But that fitness experience wasn't aimed at first at the members: I focused first on my internal customers.

I worked with my staff in a specific way to show them how to create a superior relationship with each member, one greeting and one response at a time. It was mandatory to know members' names, their stories, their goals, who they were, and what walk of life they came from. That meant my team had to be comfortable with making conversation all day long (and isn't that a clue as to the type of person you have to hire?).

My staff and I talked about the value of relationships in our work, but I also trained them on *how* to build these relationships. Over the next seven years, we created a fitness center where all the staff took a personal interest in each other and the customers. It was about having goodwill, acknowledging the presence of the other, and being interested in and connected to the members as they walked in, as they worked out, and when they left. As a result, our membership grew from eighty-eight to six hundred.

Years later, when I sold the business, I advised the new owner to continue focusing on those relationships. Alas, I learned that they took a different approach, and within the first month, membership dropped by over one hundred. It was a stark reminder of how much customer loyalty depends on a genuine, relationship-based approach.

Community is a great feeling. Our members were never for a minute just Member #27 or a membership fee. Sure, we did the transactional pieces, which are part and parcel of operating a business. But we never looked at our members as just giving us a monthly payment, not caring whether they came in or what they did when they were there. We always looked at them as people looking to fulfill a need and a purpose. We looked at our staff the same way, as people with a skill set, values, and contributions that helped people reach their goals in a friendly, supportive environment. When you treat your internal customers with service to them in mind, your sales, profits, and reputation will grow. That's a fact.

In the company I operate today, Human Power Solutions, our clients are coming to us in some part because we are able to get them grant money for some of our services. It's a two-year commitment for them. In this type of business situation, we're never guaranteed to get more business from them after two years. As of this mid-2024 writing, we've been in business for almost five years and have retained relationships with 80 percent of our clients—four out of five of them—because we have solid relationships with them. Clients who have received grant money choose to continue working with us and create budgets to hire us because we know who they are, make a point to learn their needs, and provide relevant solutions for them.

For one of those clients, I was providing some leadership development and coaching with a very small group of their people. We provided ongoing service to this small group, inviting them to give us a call when they needed support and giving them tough love when they needed it.

The company had been resistant, however, to doing more training for the rest of the organization. Members of this small group knew the company was having a hard time.

Because of the work we did and the relationship we had with the small group, they convinced their decision-makers that wider training would be a benefit. I received a call to train the rest of the staff. The relationship grew that revenue stream for us; we are helping the business grow in sustainable ways and everyone is on board to do so.

You're in a people business, and I say that without even knowing what your business is. Your entire business is founded on relationships. Transactional approaches to leading your company and your internal customers say business is all about money, but every business (and there's no getting around it) is a people business. Transactional-plus-relational approaches to leading your staff recognize that you can't have a business or profitability without relationships. Relationships create more synergy and energy for and among your internal customers. They create more trust and "stickiness" in your external customers so that they keep buying from you longer and send new customers to you willingly.

To demonstrate the dramatic differences between the transaction-only and the transactional-plus-relational holistic approach, let me talk about one of our manufacturing clients operating in the refurbishment sector. This client had three floors in their plant, and a different activity took place on each floor. There were eleven supervisors in different areas of the organization. All of these three areas sent their products to Shipping and Receiving.

Outwardly, this was a very successful company. They had lots of customers. All of their professional development focused on continuous improvement, lean methodologies, and processes (transactional training, in other words). When the owner engaged Human Power Solutions, I declined to do only process improvement training.

We worked with the supervisory staff of eleven people for about nine months and quickly learned that none of them had ever worked together even though they had all been in the same three-story building for ten to fifteen years. These supervisors had longevity with the company and yet had to admit they didn't know the people in accounting or anyone manning the phones, much less the staff on the other three production floors.

This was an Emerging Leaders program about which the owner had said, "Go ahead, but I don't think it's going to make a difference for us."

Well, it made an enormous difference. About six months into the program, one of the women was about to be fired. She was super rough around the edges and even mean to employees. During the program, however, she had an awakening of sorts. After taking a hard look at herself, she came in one day and said to my team, "I need to make a change in how I'm interacting with everybody." Her self-awareness woke up. Toward the end of the program, not only this supervisor but the others started to understand how their internal relationships were helping or hindering the workflow.

From one area to another, they agreed that with good communication, they could problem-solve together. They no longer had to escalate a problem to management. It took managers out of that hub-and-spoke structure in which every problem came to them, because now the supervisors had relationships with each other that they would leverage to resolve issues quickly. This in turn freed the managers to look at the bigger picture and move things forward.

The relationships that we built inside made the internal customers—all staff—happier and caused the company's workflow to smooth out, streamline, and even accelerate. They met each other and learned who did what in the offices and on the different production floors, which reduced the amount of misunderstanding and even conflict in the organization.

The owner admitted to me, "I wish we had spent more time on this."

People Profit

Companies investing in employee development programs have seen tangible top- and bottom-line improvements as a result, including measurable gains like these:

- 30 percent increase in employee productivity
- 25 percent reduction in customer complaints
- 40 percent reduction in call resolution time
- 30 percent increase in customer satisfaction scores (net promoter scores, or NPS)
- 24 percent higher profit than those spending less on employee development

If those numbers are not enough, organizations that provide comprehensive training can expect a *350 percent return* on their training and development investment in the long run.[1]

The average annual investment in staff development yielding returns like the ones I listed above is $1,200 per employee.[2] Your internal customers drive your profits. Invest in them.

---

[1] PsicoSmart Editorial Team, "What Are the Key Metrics for Measuring the Return on Investment in Employee Training?," Vorecol, August 28, 2024, https://psico-smart.com/en/blogs/blog-what-are-the-key-metrics-for-measuring-the-return-on-investment-in-employee-training-155677.

[2] "ATD Research: Spending on Employee Training Remains Strong," press release, Association for Talent Development, December 6, 2022, https://www.td.org/content/press-release/atd-research-spending-on-employee-training-remains-strong.

Chapter 2

Get Your (Internal) House in Order

Consider the "internal house" of your business. Your internal house consists of the departments and operating spaces of your business, the people in them, and your manner of organizing it all. You always need to assume that you can do better in all those areas, for all those internal customers.

To strengthen both the internal environment and the quality of service delivered externally, it should be no surprise by now that you must question your employees. You can't know what's not working for them, what frustrates them in carrying out their jobs, or what their potentially great ideas for improvement are unless you ask them.

Engagement Surveys

The first way to start understanding better (from your employees' perspective) what's going on inside your business is by using an *Employee Engagement Survey*. That will be your first step in figuring out what people think, what they want, and what they need.

Make no mistake: Post-COVID employees are very different from those in the pre-COVID climate. Employee expectations have shifted significantly, and thus managers, supervisors, and leaders cannot know how they have shifted without asking—and asking often.

The Psychological Contract

That you're working to get your internal house in order implies that you know what the problems, complaints, roadblocks, obstacles, and frustrations are—in your employees' view—as well as what is working well. It is the rare management team that has this information at their fingertips.

Everyone has a *psychological contract*, as Denise Rousseau described in the late 1980s–90s.[3] Rousseau is a prominent scholar in the field of organizational behavior and management. This contract represents the mutual beliefs, perceptions, and informal obligations between an employer and an employee. Employees have specific ideas about what their employers need to do for them, and conversely, employers have ideas about what they think employees need

---

[3] Denise Rousseau, "Psychological and Implied Contracts in Organizations," *Employee Responsibilities and Rights Journal*, 2 (1989): 121-139, https://doi.org/10.1007/BF01384942.

to do for the company. Often the two are very misaligned, meaning their expectations don't match.

Leaders who stay connected with the front lines of their organization get a real feel for what's going on. They see the challenges employees face—whether it's a lack of proper tools or equipment, roadblocks or too many hoops to jump through to achieve a task, or processes set up years ago that just don't work anymore. When leaders aren't aware of where the workflow is breaking down, it's tough to tackle problems, let alone fix them.

That's why the first step is simply understanding these dynamics by running an employee engagement survey. Whether you bring in an outside provider or use online resources, there are plenty of ways to get honest feedback from your team. Each person joined the team with their own skills and goals, and good leadership can help them grow, feel supported, and stay engaged by getting to know their career goals and needs as you will through the survey responses. At the end of the day, leadership makes a huge difference in shaping the experience for all employees—your internal customers.

Creating work environments where people feel purposeful and connected isn't just good for employees. It's good for the whole organization. When people feel supported, the entire team is better equipped to thrive.

Administer that survey, read all the responses with an open mind, be ready and willing to take everything to heart, and be aware that the responses might include things like:

- Only some employees have a promotion goal (but may not be clear on how to achieve that).

- Others want to fine-tune the skills they came to you with and now expand them further with company-provided training (that doesn't yet exist).

- They came with virtually no skills and perhaps no experience because it's a first job (and you knew that) and would like the organization to teach them more (but you are not).

- They're just there for the paycheck (and that's okay!).

Here's more about what to expect: Once you've run your employee engagement survey, it's likely to reveal some clear challenges with management. I hinted at a few in the above list. The feedback from employees often puts the spotlight on areas where managers are facing pressure or need support. After you've reviewed the results, the next step is to bring together your leadership team, from the CEO on down the line, and first take a close look at your ability to make immediate improvements expressed by your people.

Second, the employee engagement survey should lead you to formally assess your different leadership styles across the organization (more on that in Chapter 5). This gives you a solid foundation for understanding where strengths lie and where there's room for growth. This can be a communication assessment, a behavioral assessment, or a DiSC® assessment[4] but must be completed by all leaders—no exceptions! As with employee engagement surveys, there's a wide range of leadership assessments you can do with your managerial and executive team.

Whether for your staff or your leaders, awareness of problems precedes working out a solution to those problems. This dual survey process will cost you a little money and a bit of time to debrief, but it's a lot less expensive than losing external or internal customers because you failed to identify and then resolve problems.

And Speaking of Costs

If you're still on the fence about investing time and money in understanding how your staff really feels about your workplace, think about turnover. The cost of losing and replacing team members can be enough to knock your socks off.

Turnover isn't just about replacing one person with another in an even swap. It never is. It's a costly cycle that affects profitability in ways that aren't always visible. Each time an employee leaves, there are the immediate expenses of recruiting, hiring, onboarding, and training someone new. But the unseen costs go further: lost productivity, disrupted team dynamics, and the investment in someone who might leave before reaching their full potential.

When your turnover is high, your clients are going to feel the effects through inconsistent service, delayed

---

[4] https://www.everythingdisc.com Accessed January 8, 2025.

responses, or lack of continuity—all of which can erode trust and satisfaction over time. Never forget: Your competitors are waiting.

It takes months to break even on a new employee. If a new hire hasn't made it through your ninety-day trial period, there are still the incurred costs of that employee's salary, training, and reduced productivity while they're getting up to speed. You've lost money.[5] That's a powerful statistic for many leaders and executives.

Bad news travels faster than good news. When employees leave your business feeling dissatisfied, they share their stories with others. Potential hires often read online reviews and may choose to look elsewhere for their next job. These are just a few of the possible effects, with others worth keeping in mind as well.

Happy, Engaged Employees

The way leaders interact with employees can have a big impact on turnover, profitability, and even more so, on the company's reputation. Leadership style plays a crucial role in shaping the workplace environment and in being able to say, "We've got a happy, productive crew."

Employees are happy and engaged when they have a psychological contract that allows them to trust their employer. They know what to expect, and their employer is meeting their expectations. They have the ability and the will to go over and above their minimum job description.

---

[5] Annie Mueller, "The Cost of Hiring a New Employee," Investopedia, April 30, 2024, https://www.investopedia.com/financial-edge/0711/the-cost-of-hiring-a-new-employee.aspx.

Employees want to do purposeful work. They want to know that they're contributing, and they yearn to know how what they do fits into the bigger picture. They want to know that they're a key part of the team and that their work is valued.

This is all primarily a communication issue. How and how much does a supervisor or other company leader talk to employees? What type of actionable feedback are internal customers getting from their leaders? Employees really appreciate real-time, useful feedback. They're usually willing to make the effort to improve if the critique is clear and actionable and the way to improve is systematic or methodical enough for them to implement. A terse "You can do better" is not actionable feedback.

While annual reviews have long been the standard in the business world, checking in just once a year isn't often enough to keep everyone moving in the same direction. Annual reviews can sometimes feel negative for employees and tend to be time-consuming for managers. There's a tendency to set "performance goals" for an employee without any clue how to reach the goals (or how anyone would benefit if the goals were achieved).

Instead of that old-school approach, many organizations are moving toward real-time feedback, and the data supports why companies that provide consistent feedback experience almost 15 percent lower turnover rates, and that employees are three times more engaged when they receive regular feedback compared to those who only get annual reviews. This frequent ongoing feedback allows for quicker course corrections and creates a more engaging environment for employees.

Incorporating weekly or quarterly check-ins along with regular one-on-ones ensures that:

- The lines of communication stay open.

- Employees feel valued, heard, and trusted.

- Staff have the support and tools they need to do the work and the permission (empowerment) to act on their own in certain pre-defined instances.

- Everyone from the top-down feels aligned with the team and with the company's goals.

If you still want to do annual reviews, these ongoing check-ins make them much smoother and free of surprises since feedback has been shared along the way. By catching any issues early on—say in Q2 rather than at year's end—you give employees a chance to improve and grow in real time. The continuous feedback approach helps foster a stronger sense of belonging and commitment within the organization, keeping teams connected and performing at their best.

One thing that often comes up is that many leaders feel uneasy about regular interactions with their teams. While these conversations can be uncomfortable at first, building a culture of honest feedback ultimately strengthens trust and helps retain employees. For starters, it's helpful to support your leadership team with ongoing development in handling tough conversations, resolving conflicts constructively, and digging into the root of any issue. With frequent follow-ups and performance check-ins, feedback becomes more of a natural conversational process rather than something confrontational. Leaders also benefit from honing skills in critical thinking, creative problem-solving, and effective communication, thus creating a supportive environment where employees feel genuinely engaged. By involving employees in the creative process, you encourage them to help shape solutions, making them active participants in improving the workplace.

One of the divides between leaders and internal customers stems from the reluctance to state why.

"Why do it this new way, boss?"

"Because it will be better."

This type of vague response is not a reason. Without understanding why the change is happening, employees will conclude it doesn't make sense, and you won't have their buy-in. They may even ignore you! Explain your thinking and ask for their thoughts. Many times, they will have a better way to do it than the whole leadership team missed—after all, this is work they do for the business all day. Listening to their proposed solutions is also what feedback is all about. Being willing and able to explain the reason something is happening or your thought process behind the change will help your employees embrace it. It's human to resist change, and it's a leader's job to lift that resistance through understanding. We understand each other by talking.

When they follow this process of listening to employees' perspectives and making employees a part of solutions, our clients experience the dual benefit of having happy, engaged internal customers:

- When they need to hire, their current employees willingly recommend new people to them, because they like the culture that has spread throughout the organization and want to share their "great place to work."

- When happy and engaged frontline people talk to external customers, that engagement is felt through more effective service; a more cheerful, involved manner; and more relationship-building efforts. External customers come back again and again, and they bring new business as well.

Disgruntled Employees

It is not just disgruntled clients posting bad reviews far and wide across the web that can sink you. A disgruntled employee can give your company bad reviews that will spread like wildfire, too. Remember that bad news moves faster than good. Sometimes a disgruntled employee is unmotivated and just unhappy at the thought of having to work anywhere, and, yes, this happens in every organization. This type of employee is there to collect a paycheck, and that's fine. Just be sure those employees are doing their jobs, keeping their heads down, and not creating conflict or difficulties.

The other side of disgruntlement is the toxic employee. They're competitive or even gleeful about sabotaging other people and their work, and they take pleasure in besmirching reputations—the list can be long. Be very aware that sometimes your leaders are the toxic employees.

It's important to dig deep and get to the root of any discontent. Is it tied to leadership? Is it an internal customer challenge that's affecting the whole team's experience?

Let me share an example of how a toxic leader can impact employee engagement. A colleague of mine teaches a graduate-level course on Employee Engagement where they introduce the concept of psychological contracts—those unwritten expectations between employers and employees which often shift from job to job. One student shared his own experience with this.

He had worked at a tax firm in a data-heavy role that involved repetitive tasks with little communication or mentorship from leadership. Although he was passionate about numbers, the tax code, and finance, the lack of growth opportunities left him feeling detached from the business and the people in it. Eventually, he moved to a different firm with a completely different culture. This new company invested in his development, encouraging continuous learning and even covering his master's degree tuition. They frequently checked in on his goals and involved him in community service initiatives. That created the very opposite environment for him from his prior job: He felt a sense of belonging. The difference was night and day. Now he feels valued, energized, and empowered to bring ideas to his managers who genuinely listen.

Although he's still early in his career, the supportive environment makes him feel more than just "Employee #107." This experience highlights how leadership, culture, and communication can make all the difference in an employee's sense of fulfillment and loyalty.

When leaders aren't tuned in to their people or they've let their ego get in the way, it's easy to overlook just how essential employees really are. Think of them as your internal customers; they're the lifeblood of your success. Losing talented people isn't just about turnover. Keep in mind that unhappy employees don't just leave; they leave a lasting impact on both your bottom line and how your organization is seen out there.

Have you ever been waiting in a checkout line, stuck listening to disgruntled employees as they trash (that's the technical term!) their company? My sister and her husband were at a big-box store that shall remain unnamed. They were waiting in line at the customer service counter to return an item, but the employees behind the counter weren't paying attention to them. They had to stand there listening to two people talk about the fact that they weren't getting paid time and a half for this holiday and how it wasn't fair.

These employees were speaking very poorly about the company right in front of the customers. It wasn't so much that they weren't getting the extra pay (which is potentially a legal issue). It was the fact that they had *not* been trained to *not* talk about this sort of topic in front of customers. They didn't have that personal self-awareness and showed a very negative side of their own personalities to strangers.

We've all probably experienced this in a retail business where employees are just numbers and are just marking time. Instead of being valuable and valued contributors, they're just "warm bodies" assigned because the store manager needed the spots filled.

Those Reviews

Another way to get your internal house in order is by taking a look at what's being said about your business online. Your internal and external reputation can take a few hits that might fly under the radar if you're not actively looking for feedback.

Platforms like Glassdoor let employees leave anonymous reviews, giving you a peek into how people really feel or felt about working there. Glassdoor is a really important ongoing internal reality check on your business. If you don't have any reviews on Glassdoor and you've got some really happy employees, ask them to post their thoughts, reminding them that it's anonymous. There's nothing wrong with doing that.

A great number of reviews just talk about an employee's experience working at a company. Those reviews then become part of your brand and your external reputation. However, use Glassdoor reviews as a learning moment for your leadership. If you see negative reviews or comments, take them to heart. Try to honestly assess whether you have a true problem. Remember, you can't fix a problem that you haven't identified, so don't get defensive and don't procrastinate about taking action.

Another type of outstanding review you can legitimately solicit is from your customers' responses to a direct survey, which can provide your business with a NPS.[6] The NPS is a survey metric asking respondents to rate the likelihood that they would recommend a company, product, or service to others. It has been used with success by tens of thousands of businesses in every industry you can name and helps them all make continuous internal improvements. Contrary to the Glassdoor reviews, the direct recipient of the NPS survey is, of course, your individual external customer.

You can also cast a wider net by Googling your company name and looking at your reviews from the perspective of the outside world. What actions will you take to improve things once you've read them all? They say knowledge is power, but the knowledge you gain by reading internal and

---

[6] You can use a dedicated NPS software or a customer experience management platform for easy setup.

external reviews is only considered power if you act on it. Don't go into denial. Don't procrastinate. Make the changes.

People Profit

On average, it can take up to six months for new hires—from entry-level to mid-management level—to reach their expected performance levels. During the first four weeks, new employees function at only about 25 percent productivity.

For midrange positions, the cost to replace an employee is around 20 percent of their annual salary. When it comes to replacing people in executive positions, costs may reach up to 213 percent of their average salary.[7]

The costs to reach peak productivity and to replace employees should be reason enough to recruit wisely and develop continuously. In the next chapters, we'll look at how to do more of that.

---

[7] Levi Olmstead, "The Cost of Onboarding New Employees in 2024 (+Calculator)," Whatfix blog, March 16, 2022, https://whatfix.com/blog/cost-of-onboarding.

Chapter 3

Employees Are Your Biggest Asset

Take a moment to ask yourself what you really know about the people on your team. You might have someone who's fluent in Swedish or Korean, a marathon winner, or a volunteer literacy coach. Maybe there's a father of eleven kids or a couple of young employees who spend all their free time volunteering at the local food bank. But chances are you don't even know if you have amazing people like this, because you've never asked.

Many leaders tend to see employees as just warm bodies—a term and a practice I really dislike. You hire someone to fill a role, especially in fields like hospitality or retail, where it might be their first job, and they don't stay long. Then turnover hits, and you're back to recruiting, filling one spot just to lose another soon after.

But what if, as a leader, you shifted your perspective? Instead of seeing these employees as temporary hires, what if you viewed them as the lifeblood of your business, adding real value for however long they're with you?

Is There a Career Path?

Sometimes, employees might just see their job as a way to collect a paycheck—they're not necessarily thinking about a career path. Even if that's their perspective, what if you still looked at them as one of your valuable assets? They might be excellent at the role you hired them for, and with that kind of contribution, they could end up staying for years. In its own way, that's a version of a career, isn't it?

For however long they're with you, it's worth investing in their development. When employees feel supported and skilled, they're more likely to represent your brand well and deliver great service. Helping them reach their full potential can boost both their effectiveness and their pride in their work.

We realize that some of the roles in our companies don't need formal education, but they do require specific skills. You probably have team members who didn't come from formal training but still need those skills to succeed in their jobs. Why wait until the end of their ninety-day probation to see if they'll "make it"? Instead of leaving them to sink or swim, start investing in their development from day one. Training often focuses on job tasks, which is essential, but what if you went further? Imagine if onboarding included personal development through helping employees strengthen communication skills, understanding their own work style, and connecting with others. By supporting them as people, not just workers, you can help them see the potential for growth, both with your company and in their careers. Starting this from the beginning can make a huge difference in their success and satisfaction.

Here's a true story about a banker I work with. College wasn't the right path for her, but instead of closing doors, her employer opened them. They showed her what was possible, guiding her on the skills she'd need to grow within the company. With that support, she didn't just advance. She flourished, eventually becoming a vice president and leading a large team. The impact? She's not just more skilled; she's more confident, more loyal, and deeply invested in the bank's success. This kind of support didn't just create a leader ready and able to create more success stories in those she trains; it created a dedicated advocate for the organization. When employees see a clear path and know they have your support, it can change everything.

Here's something we don't often ask in the workplace, although it comes up all the time at home: Why are you here? Why do you come to work each day? For some people, the job is just about paying the bills—they haven't thought much beyond that. But that's actually a great opportunity to find out if they're looking for something more long-term. If they are, that's your chance to show them what your organization has to offer and how they can grow with you. A simple question can open the door to a bigger conversation about their future and help them see the possibilities ahead.

Even employees who might just be working to pay the bills could end up building a long-term career with you if they see opportunities for growth and development. Sometimes, a career path starts simply with the chance for stability and the feeling of being valued. When you invest in their development, employees are far more likely to stay.

It is tough to cultivate growth if employees feel like "warm bodies"—interchangeable or disposable. Imagine trying to sit and stand at the same time; it's impossible. In the same way, employees can sense whether they're seen as valued individuals or just another cog in the wheel. When people are treated as unique assets with skill and potential, they're more motivated to bring their best to the organization. Without this sense of value, many will leave before you've even had a chance to see all they're capable of contributing.

Turnover can't be avoided entirely, but its impact on your business is significant, and your approach to employees makes a real difference. Creating an environment where employees feel seen, heard, and purposeful can go a long way toward keeping turnover below industry averages. Instead of thriving at the expense of your team, you can become a company that prospers by supporting and investing in your people as individuals with potential. Now, they are not just employees, but unique assets who grow with you.

Make Recruitment and Retention Easier

If you're in retail, banking, manufacturing, or a field where you have labor positions, finding and holding on to employees is very difficult. This is a transient environment in which employees jump from job to job. However, once you have a policy and reputation for working with your employees on their professional development and helping them to create a career path, along with striving to find out about the skills and potential they bring to your business, the word gets out.

One of my clients told me an older story about working with the Swedish Embassy on a project. Inadvertently, the embassy sent a document in Swedish rather than English. The project manager (PM) wanted to look effective and hesitated to call them for the translation (this was before everyone had Google Translate at their fingertips). The PM asked around the team, and it turned out that one of them was pretty good with German and could extrapolate enough of the foreign document to guide the PM. Hooray for internal customers with a wide range of (surprising) skills! There was much congratulatory laughter and kudos given for the effort.

The PM had learned a valuable lesson about leading a team: His employees were huge assets with hidden skills. He made a point to ask everyone what their hidden talent was at the next team meeting. He never hesitated again to ask his team for a rarely needed skill—and someone always seemed to step up.

Your whole goal is to become best-in-class for the professional development of your employees. If you have employees who are talking publicly about their very positive experience with a company that cares about them as people, or a company that cares about their skills and their career potential, you're going to have people knocking on your door. Once word gets out (and it always does) that you take career goals and internal professional development seriously, you should see prospective employees come knocking. The word on the street should be "Sorry, if you don't know someone in the company, you're not going to get in." Your jobs should become much in demand.

When company leaders talk about struggling with recruitment and retention, there's usually a story behind it—and it often leads back to internal culture and employee satisfaction. Let's be honest: New hires don't just want a desk and a to-do list. They want to feel like they're part of something from day one: Was their welcome memorable or did they get the "Here's your workstation, good luck!" treatment?

Hiring someone is more than just filling a role; it's about helping everyone see a future with your company. That means more than just teaching them the tasks; it's about showing them where they fit in, giving them a sense of purpose, and building those connections that make work enjoyable. After all, people stick around for more than a paycheck—they stay for the sense of belonging and the appreciation of their efforts and for a clear path for growth.

Social onboarding is just as important as job training. Because if they're excited to be part of the team, they're way more likely to stick around for the long haul. So maybe it's time to rethink onboarding as more of a "welcome to the family" experience than a checklist. Trust me, a little enthusiasm and investment here can go a long way!

Not a Farm: No Silos

Another key to a well-functioning team (and ultimately to happy clients and a healthy bottom line) is avoiding silos in your company. Take the restaurant industry as an example. You've got dishwashers, cooks, busboys, servers, and bartenders, each with specific roles. But hierarchies can develop here too, and often, the bartenders see themselves at the top, rarely considering what happens if the dishwasher doesn't show up. Without teamwork, this "It's not my job" attitude can lead to breakdowns in service.

Cross-training can be a game-changer here. By giving everyone the chance to understand each role, you create a team that's not only more resilient but also more empathetic. Imagine the bartender spending a shift at the dishwasher station during peak hours; they quickly realize the level of skill and efficiency needed to keep things running. The server who spends time behind the bar discovers that bartending is more than pouring drinks; it's managing multiple orders, reading the room, and keeping up with everyone's tab, all often under pressure.

This kind of empathy and respect strengthens the entire team. When everyone sees the value (and challenges) of each role, they're more willing to pitch in when things get rough. That "all-hands-on-deck" willingness directly impacts the client experience—customers notice when a team is in sync, and they feel the difference in quality and consistency. Plus, this harmony boosts productivity and lowers turnover, which means better profits. Ultimately, a connected, well-trained team isn't just nice to have; it's an investment in employee retention, as well as in your company's reputation and profitability.

It's not just in the corporate and traditional business world that cross-training is vital for your internal customer. Think of pro sports, in which football legends spend hours a week in dance, Pilates, or yoga classes. Think of Broadway, where producers and directors search high and low for the (cross-trained) triple-threat performer who can act, sing, and dance. Think, too, of the military, where the US Army Special Forces (a.k.a. the Green Berets) or US Navy Seals are all cross-trained in each other's special skill in case one of them is out of commission.

In pro sports, the players are multimillion-dollar assets of the team owner. That cross-training protects them from injury. In the performing arts, the so-called triple-threat performers can take on a wider scope of projects and roles and attract a broader audience to a production (improving the producer's bottom line). In the military, the teams can keep on mission when each one has a wider scope of skills to achieve success.

My husband is a former Army Airborne. On his team were the gunner and the tank driver. Each man needed to know everything the other two knew to complete missions. They were deployed to Somalia, Honduras, and other dangerous places in the world. This team needed to understand the orders, know their jobs inside and out, and most of all keep a focus on the overall mission goal. If one person didn't know what to do in a given situation, they would all be dead—literally. This is an extreme example. They had each other's backs, and although they've been out of the army for a while now, they still get together and talk about the times they were shot at and their other "adventures" (I shudder to imagine them) on the job. Their bond is strong.

Cross-training treats your team members as true assets by broadening their skill and understanding of the business. When employees see the bigger picture, they're more able to situate their own role as the whole and be more engaged as a result. They are more likely to stay with the company. It's not just about retention, though—it's also about resilience. In real life, snarl-ups happen. Someone is out sick, the system goes down, a needed order is held up across the country. Having a team that can adapt keeps everything running smoothly.

In many companies, the value of cross-training is often overlooked. It's a simple approach that sends a powerful message: When employees see that leadership believes in their ability to fill different roles (even briefly), they feel more valued and empowered. Imagine an employee thinking, "Oh, they trust me to handle this, too? That's great!" Their cross-training makes them feel capable and ready to step up when needed. It doesn't mean they're expected to do everything all the time, but knowing they can help out when necessary, gives a real sense of pride and accomplishment.

Cross-training can also break down silos and level the playing field across roles. When employees understand each other's responsibilities, it reduces the notion of "untouchable" jobs or the feeling of "The place couldn't survive without me." Everyone becomes part of a unified team where each person's contribution matters. Sure, people will still have their specialties but having others who can pitch in creates a more resilient, responsive, and supportive environment.

This idea goes beyond simply learning tasks. It's also about shifting perspectives. It's about protecting the business (and, frankly, each other's jobs). Most people don't consider a restaurant dishwasher's role in the dining experience. The job might seem unglamorous, but it's essential to the entire operation. A single dirty plate that goes unnoticed by the dishwasher, then by the cook during plate-up, and last by a harried server, has an impact. When the disappointed diner is the only one who sees the dirty plate, it can lead to immediate complaints, requests for manager intervention, not to mention other diners wondering what the problem is. Not only that, a dirty plate incident (however it was handled) might still earn you a bad review. You've lost the diner's trust . . . and lost his future business.

When each person understands the ripple effect of their role, they're more likely to step up, be diligent, and watch out for one another. It's not just about completing tasks; it's about quality assurance and having each other's backs.

Cross-training helps build a culture of mutual respect and understanding. When employees know what goes into each other's jobs, they recognize each other's challenges and genuinely want to make one another look good. It's an environment where everyone is invested in the success of the whole team. And in the end, that's what drives better service, stronger teamwork, and a lasting sense of pride and loyalty.

I joined Chili's back in 1995, before they were a franchise when they were part of Brinker International, a company that set a bar high in hospitality. They didn't just offer jobs; they offered careers. Coming in as a new manager with four years at Marriott under my belt, I thought I knew what I was doing. Spoiler alert: I didn't. Brinker's training program had other plans for me.

As part of my manager's training, I had to spend two weeks in every role. Dishwashing, cooking, serving, bartending, hosting, bussing—you name it, I did it. And let's just say my ego got a serious reality check. I went in thinking I was the best thing since sliced bread, but after two weeks of scrubbing dishes and running orders, I quickly learned to set my ego aside.

Now, here's the funny part. I wasn't humbled by the kitchen part. I cooked my way through college and loved the heat of the kitchen. But serving and bartending? Not exactly in my comfort zone. The pressure was more intense, and I didn't love it. Still, Brinker's approach gave me the confidence and skills to step in when needed, even if it wasn't my favorite task. That empowerment was worth every shift.

This cross-training didn't help just me. It built a team around me that trusted me to step up (and to know how). They knew that if things got crazy busy, I was not going to be barking orders and waving my hands around. I could (and did) jump in, take a table, bring out drinks, or clear a table without hesitation. They saw I was right there with them, and I knew they'd do the same. Our joint efforts paid off, too. We consistently earned five-star reviews, aced our mystery shopper events, and achieved top scores in friendliness, timeliness, and overall guest experience.

In the end, it wasn't just a training program; it was a lesson in teamwork, humility, and showing up for each other. I have Brinker to thank for it.

What Is This "Valuing" Thing?

I can't stress enough the importance of valuing your employees, even if they're only with you for a short time and not necessarily looking for a lifelong career with your company. You don't often hear objections to the idea of "valuing employees," but let's take a closer look at what that really means.

We've all heard the stories about employees leaving because they didn't feel valued. According to countless media reports, feeling undervalued is often at the heart of why people choose to leave a job. For employees, feeling valued means knowing that their leaders genuinely see them as individuals. It means knowing their boss is curious about who they are, what drives them, what skills and talents and experience they possess from prior jobs, and what makes them excited to come to work *here* each day. In other words, the boss talks and listens to them. It's about feeling recognized as a person, not just a warm body on a six-hour shift.

For leaders, valuing employees isn't just about knowing their names; it's about understanding their goals and motivations. When leaders take the time to learn what their team members are aiming for, they can create development opportunities that genuinely support those aspirations. This kind of support goes beyond a paycheck. It's about showing that you're dedicated to their growth, offering ways for them to expand their skills and grow along a career path. It's a win-win: Employees feel valued, and in turn, their contributions help drive the success of the business.

When I first started working, there was a popular phrase for certain managers' style: MBWA, or "managing by walking around." These leaders would actually leave the comfort of their corner offices to roam the floors, check in with employees to have a real talk, and get a firsthand feel of what was happening. Imagine that! Managers stepping out, chatting with people who might otherwise only see them in the company newsletter! It wasn't just a breath of fresh air; it was a way to build connections and show employees they were seen, heard, and respected as part of the team.

And here's the magic of that: When employees feel and see their value to the company (and their manager), they begin to see themselves as assets, real contributors to the success of the business. This sense of being valued and valuable becomes contagious; it spreads to how employees treat each other and extends right to your customers who feel it, too. It's hard not to notice when an employee is happy to be there, genuinely helpful, and proud of the work they do. In the end, these are people who bring real value and profit to the company, because they care about it as much as you do.

Unfortunately, in too many companies, employees barely get a glimpse of the CEO or owner. When there's little or no interaction, it can start to feel like "us versus them," and that divide isn't exactly helping anyone feel valued. A simple "walkabout" can change all that. Just a few minutes of MBWA, that managing by walking around, can make a big difference. A quick check-in, asking how things are going or whether there's anything they need, and maybe even rolling up your sleeves once in a while are ways to show employees that they're important to you.

I witnessed the founding CEO of an insurance company doing some MBWA. He went to say hello to a group of temp workers, hired to stuff envelopes in a back room for a marketing campaign. One of the temps said to him, "Hi. So, what's your job here?" She had no idea who he was. While some were stifling laughter, I realized (as did the CEO) that she didn't know him at all and was genuinely curious. He sat down right next to her at the table and began stuffing envelopes and while he did, told her his job. She was fascinated rather than intimidated, and his regular staff was deeply impressed with his approach. She was not just a temp to him but an important factor in getting his marketing campaign out. And who knows? She may have ended up buying some of his company's insurance!

Here's the best part: When leaders step out of the office to meet people where they're at, the workplace culture shifts. Suddenly, everyone's on the same page, pulling together toward a common goal. Employees feel more connected and respected, and that connection shows up in the work, the interactions with customers, and ultimately in the bottom line. It's amazing what a few extra steps around the workplace can do, not just for morale but for creating a culture where people want to stick around, do great work, and keep driving the business forward.

The Cost of Turnover

Wondering if cross-training or a professional development program is worth the cost? It's a fair question. Those programs aren't free, after all. But for a little reality check, compare that investment to what turnover costs you every time an employee leaves because they felt like just another cog in the wheel. Guess what? It's a lot more than you think.

Studies show it takes about five months just to break even on a new hire. If an employee doesn't make it through their first ninety days, you're already in the red. And that doesn't even cover the hidden costs—the time spent recruiting, interviewing, training, and then doing it all over again when the next hire comes in. It's a revolving door that gets expensive fast.

If you want a real eye-opener, look at your own turnover figures. Crunching those numbers might feel a bit like checking the fridge after the holidays, but it's worth it. You'll see just how much those early exits are costing, which might make a well-structured developed program look like a smart investment. At the end of the day, developing your team can be a win-win: Employees feel valued, they're more likely to stick around, and your company avoids that costly turnover cycle. Now, that's a return on investment worth smiling about!

People Profit

Lacking any visible or tangible career path, as was discussed at the start of this chapter, is the primary reason employees leave companies. Adding professional development for every employee gives them a sense that you want them for the longer term (a "career") and are willing to develop them to grow within the organization or to take on greater responsibilities.

Nearly a quarter (24 percent) of all employee departures occur because they can't perceive any future opportunities in the organization. Most employees want to advance their careers and learn new skills. Laying out a potential path from the very beginning of their employment with you can have long-term benefits, not the least of which is retention.[8]

Those statements of mine come notably from Joey Coleman's research of companies worldwide, which also found that 50 percent of hourly employees quit before their one-hundred-day anniversary, while 20 percent of non-hourly or salaried employees quit before then.[9]

LinkedIn's *Workplace Learning Report* indicates that 94 percent of employees would stay longer if they were offered learning and development opportunities,[10] and 86 percent say they would switch jobs for one with more chances to grow (through a career path with professional development).[11]

Whether you're just starting to explore professional development for your team or already have some effort underway, it's worth reflecting on how it's going. Investing in

---

[8] Shep Hyken, "The Real Reasons Employees Stay or Leave," *Forbes*, July 9, 2023, https://www.forbes.com/sites/shephyken/2023/07/09/beyond-money-the-real-reasons-employees-stay-or-leave.

[9] Coleman's two books, *Never Lose a Customer Again* (Portfolio/Penguin, 2018) and *Never Lose an Employee Again* (Portfolio/Penguin 2023), review his research.

[10] Benjamin Spar, Colleen Dye, Rachel Lefkowitz, and Deanna Pate, *2018 Workplace Learning Report* (LinkedIn Learning, 2018), https://learning.linkedin.com/resources/workplace-learning-report-2018.

[11] Erica Keswin, "3 Ways to Boost Retention Through Professional Development," April 5, 2022, https://hbr.org/2022/04/3-ways-to-boost-retention-through-professional-development.

your internal customers can lower turnover, boost retention, and energize employees in their daily roles. If you haven't started yet, or if your current approach isn't delivering the results you'd hoped for, now is the perfect time to take a fresh look and consider the next steps.

Chapter 4

Choosing the Right Manager

If you're an executive of a company looking at promoting someone to a management or leadership position, there are three things to think about.

First, consider the current dynamics of today's marketplace, particularly when it comes to levels of formal education. Diplomas don't always need to be a criterion for selection. What matters is what a potential employee knows and how effective they are at understanding and performing the required work.

Second, you'll want to examine your promotion candidates for strong emotional intelligence (sometimes called EQ, an emotional version of IQ).[12] EQ is a skill that improves a person's ability to connect with other people. This is a skill that managers, without a doubt, will find essential in every situation (and yes, it can be learned).

Third, you should take time to understand the real differences between a manager and a leader—and which one you really need. Each brings unique skills and qualities to the table, and they're not always interchangeable. Not every manager is a leader, not every leader is suited to be a manager. Recognizing these differences is essential when deciding who to promote into a manager's role. So, what sets managers and leaders apart?

Leaders

There is no doubt that to survive, thrive, and grow the business, you need one or more people in the cockpit who have a wide, long view of the market and the company's place in it. It's important to cultivate forward-thinking leaders and build a pipeline of talent-focused leaders, not just for the next year but for the next decade.

Leaders are the ones who see the bigger picture. They're at the helm, looking ahead to the horizon with a clear vision for growth, adaptability, and long-term success. While rooted in the present, they're always focused on finding ways to improve and move the organization forward.

---

[12] Lauren Landry, "Why Emotional Intelligence Is Important in Leadership," Harvard Business School, April 3, 2019, https://online.hbs.edu/blog/post/emotional-intelligence-in-leadership.

Effective leaders have a clear understanding of the business's mission, goals, and the values that guide daily operations. They excel at working with people, balancing the needs of internal customers with the company's broader vision and the expectations of external customers.

Great leadership doesn't necessarily require mastery of every task or a close connection to every individual. What matters is their ability to recognize which skills are being utilized, identify the people who hold key knowledge, and bring those elements together to think strategically about the department or organization.

Leaders are the ones stepping back to ask and answer critical questions about resources, finances, and the decisions that shape the future of the business. They are the ones asking and answering the money and resource questions that wrap around issues such as:

1. How can we get better, more efficient and effective, more profitable?

2. What are our newest, biggest advantages or threats in the marketplace and how do we best approach both so that the business thrives?

Managers

If leaders are at the helm of the business to guide it through economic waters, managers are at the head of functions being performed inside the business. Managers are the boots-on-the-ground people who are running a department or a functional team. They know all the tasks and processes involved in whatever their department does and make sure that it's all getting done.

There's no doubt that you need to have managers supervising the teams that perform the day-to-day work that gets your product out to consumers. Without managers, your processes, quality controls, communications, and accounting don't get rolled out properly or on time. As managers focus on the daily tasks and project timelines, they are the ones responsible for your staffing and have a direct relationship with all your employees. The following are other unique roles and responsibilities of managers:

1. They are process and timeline-focused, being sure the team gets the daily tasks done—they are the ones to motivate and guide employees to doing the tasks.

2. They need high levels of interpersonal skills because they have direct relationships and interactions with employees. They are the ones communicating good and bad news, correcting performance issues along the way, and making sure everyone has the tools and resources they need to perform.

3. They create the daily atmosphere or vibe of your workplace.

Choosing for EQ

Managers play a key role in your employees' performance and, ultimately, in your business's success. Great interpersonal skills are essential for this role, and that means a high level of emotional intelligence (EQ). If they don't have it already, they can absolutely develop it.

When it comes to EQ, some people seem to have a natural talent for it. They can read the room, truly listen, and pick up on the unspoken messages in conversations. They know how to make adjustments to motivate their team and keep things moving smoothly. But EQ *is* a teachable skill and one that can be improved with time and practice.

Why does EQ matter so much? Because managers, supervisors, foremen, and team leaders with strong EQ tend to get the best out of their teams. They inspire higher engagement, boost productivity, and foster better communication and collaboration. When managers are great listeners and truly understand their teams, employees feel heard, and that connection drives better results for everyone.

What does a person learn from EQ training? EQ is typically broken down into four core competencies: self-awareness, self-management, social awareness, and relationship management. The core competencies guide leaders and managers in understanding their team members' motivations, needs, behaviors, and more. EQ in fact enhances several skills:

- You become more adept at recognizing and managing your emotions and those of your team members.

- You improve your ability to listen so that you can ask relevant new questions to acquire more information and respond appropriately.

- You gain new understanding and connection that allows you to motivate your team members in a way that gets positive action and buy-in from each one.[13]

To get started right away, you can take EQ assessments online to find out where you are on the Emotional Intelligence scale.[14] There are also many workshops available to help strengthen areas where you might need improvement.

Your business thrives when it has both leaders and managers. *Leaders focus on guiding the business toward long-term success* while *managers ensure tasks are completed on time and with precision.* Both play critical roles, navigating through good times, challenges, and periods of disruption to keep things moving forward.

---

[13] Matt Tenney, "The Impact of Emotional Intelligence in Leadership on Employee Performance," Business Leadership Today, accessed September 23, 2024, https://businessleadershiptoday.com/how-emotional-intelligence-of-leaders-can-enhance-employee-performance.

[14] Just type "EQ assessment free" into your browser for many viable options.

Promoting the Right One

Understanding the difference between leaders and managers is essential, especially when it comes to promotions. Promoting the wrong person can be costly, not just in lost productivity and revenue but also in the trust of your internal and external customers. Too often people are promoted because they are great at their job, with no consideration of whether they have people skills.

Maybe you've seen this before—a high-performing employee is promoted into leadership because "they know the job inside and out," yet they've never connected with coworkers in any meaningful way. They have never helped out in a tough moment. Suddenly, the star worker is in a leadership role where they're expected to guide and inspire others. As a result, they struggle—and so does the entire team. The team loses a top performer and gains a manager who isn't equipped to lead.

This is why emotional intelligence is so critical. Managers need more than technical skills. They need the ability to give constructive feedback, have tough conversations, and motivate their team. Without strong interpersonal skills, even the most productive worker can falter in a leadership role. Start developing EQ early so that when promotions happen, candidates are ready for the demands of the role.

Managers are what I call the "feet on the street" and they shape the atmosphere on the floor. They're not just overseeing production; they're building the team culture. They help employees see how their work connects to the bigger picture, whether it's reducing waste, improving safety, or ensuring quality. Imagine a manager at that company I told you about that makes knee replacement parts saying, "This could be for your mom, your grandparent, or even you." That's the kind of connection that inspires pride and purpose.

Great managers are present. They're in the trenches with their team, understanding the work and the people behind it. They're the ones who celebrate successes, uncover what went wrong, and ensure every employee feels seen and valued. For all these needs, before promoting someone, ask if they have the skills to connect, communicate, and lead. If not, are you ready to help them get there? These are the traits that make a good manager and, ultimately, drive your business forward.

Finding the Unlikely Leader

Sometimes, the best managers come from the most unexpected places. They may not be your most technically skilled employees, but they excel at working with people. They know how to motivate, inspire, and bring a team together to get the job done. That's the real key to effective management.

This is why promoting your most skilled worker isn't always the best move. Remember, a manager's role isn't about doing the work themselves. It's about guiding and empowering others to do it. Great managers know how to communicate effectively, explain the "why" behind tasks, and motivate their team to see the bigger picture.

To choose the right manager, focus on the person who's naturally good with people. It might not be the person who produces the most widgets or clocks the fastest times, but it could be the one who steps in to help a frazzled coworker or explains a tricky process to a new hire with clarity and patience. This is the person who keeps the team calm and focused when things go wrong. This is the one who says, "We've got this. Let's pull together one more time." They're the glue that holds the group together, creating a positive environment where everyone feels supported and motivated to give their best.

Don't overlook these individuals when considering promotions. They might not be the first person who comes to mind, but their ability to foster teamwork and keep morale high makes them invaluable. They're the ones who can rally the team during tough times, ensure the work gets done, and that everyone feels like part of a shared success. Give these "unlikely leaders" a closer look. They just might surprise you.

Create Energy

At Marriott, Chili's, and now Human Power Solutions, fun has always been a core value. Some managers and leaders might dismiss "fun" as frivolous and unsuited for the workplace but let me tell you that it's anything but. Creating an environment where work feels enjoyable and even lighthearted can make all the difference, especially during high-pressure shifts or high-sales seasons.

If every workday feels like a pressure cooker, how long will it take your team to burn out? Exhaustion takes over, motivation dwindles, and suddenly, showing up doesn't feel worth it anymore. But when there's room for laughter and moments of joy, even the toughest days feel a little more manageable.

At Chili's, my team and I would close the restaurant at 1:00 a.m. knowing full well many would be back on the floor at 10:00 a.m. that same morning. It was tough. People were dragging, tired from the late nights and early starts. As their manager, I saw it as my job to create an atmosphere that made those long days a little easier. My goal wasn't just to get through the shift but to inject some energy and fun into it for everyone.

You have to remember that customers don't know or care that you're tired at the start of a shift. They've come for an experience, and they expect you to deliver. I took that to heart, knowing that if I could lift the team's spirit, that energy would naturally flow to the customers. One of my favorite ways to do this was by introducing contests. We'd put a bingo card on the chalkboard with challenges like, "Let's see who can sell the most margaritas" or "Let's pitch those two new appetizers."

It wasn't about hard sales targets at all. Instead, it was about creating moments of friendly, informal competition that made work feel less like work. I'll never forget one waiter who shouted with a huge smile and a little dancing jig, "Third margarita in twenty minutes, guys!" His enthusiasm was infectious, and it rippled through the team. Even the kitchen staff were laughing and got in on the fun, cheering each other on. It wasn't just hitting numbers; it wasn't even about the numbers. It was about creating a positive, engaged atmosphere where everyone felt lifted.

Playing to Strengths

Good managers don't have to be good at everything, but they do need to recognize and leverage the strengths of their team. What are their strengths? Ask! Observe!

I'll admit that I wasn't the most detail-oriented manager back then. Inventory? Not my strong suit. But I knew who to turn to when I needed help. I leaned on my shift leads and team members who thrived on the details I struggled with. They, in turn, relied on me for my strengths—my ability to motivate, bring order to chaos, and create a culture of collaboration. For me, it was about knowing when to step back and let others shine while focusing on what I did best: building relationships and energizing the group.

Contrasting Styles

Not every manager at the restaurant had the same approach. There was another manager, an industry veteran, who had a different style. He was task-driven, highly structured, and leaned toward micromanagement. While I respected that everyone brought their own style to leadership, his approach often felt rigid and overly critical.

Word traveled fast among the team. Employees started asking when he was scheduled and requesting time off when they knew they'd be working with him. His focus on tasks over people created tension, and while he eventually noticed the impact, his efforts to change didn't impress the team at all. He began mimicking some of the techniques our general manager and I used—cheerleading, creating contests, even smiling more—but it didn't come naturally to him. It felt forced, and the team could sense it. What I took away from that set of observations wasn't that his style was inherently wrong. It was that authenticity matters. Leadership isn't about copying what works for someone else. It's about finding your own rhythm and connecting with your team in a way that makes it feel genuine. If you're not being authentic, people will see through it, and the connection you're trying to build will fall flat. The need for genuine connection with the staff you're managing is universal.

My Chili's example is in the food industry, but one manufacturing company that we worked with had team leads and supervisors who were very task-oriented. Many of those leaders just didn't understand the impact their words had on their workers.

We guided them through behavioral and EQ training, including an entire continuous improvement initiative. The company invested in courses that covered management of difficult conversations and conflict mediation, too, without which the improvement initiative would not have been successful. After about nine months, we were able to positively change the whole emotional, behavioral, and performance undercurrent for that group. It was a whole new workplace. According to their feedback, it almost felt like a whole new workforce.

The biggest impact the process had on the workers came from seeing that the company had invested in them. They were excited that the leadership team had seriously invested in their growth and development. Several of the managers hadn't finished high school, and others had some vocational school, but they all had a lot of life education. It made a big difference in their own work satisfaction and in the contributions they could make to others moving forward. The empathy—that real connection among the workers—along with a keen understanding of the inner workings of the company made for an extremely smooth transition.

New perspectives and perceptions are an outcome of the professional development investment, right alongside improved effectiveness in all areas of your business.

People Profit

It's never a waste of money to invest in professional development for your managers and leaders. It's never wasted effort to examine whether your candidate for promotion is the right fit.

Gallup research found that when they're hiring managers, "companies fail to choose the candidate with the right talent for the job 82 percent of the time."[15] That's four out of five times!

It's a common mistake and a costly one, since staff quits (or threatens to quit) because their managers fail them by not investing in their growth, furthering their career in any way, or acknowledging their contributions to the business.[16] The time it takes to hire managers has increased by 18 percent since the COVID-19 pandemic.

Hiring the wrong manager means you'll be spending valuable time and money to fill the role again. In that management void, your business could be losing external customers, but your internal customers could be getting more and more frustrated at having no leadership. All the while you're recruiting, you find yourself hoping that your staff productivity will remain high and that they don't resign en masse while you get your manager's recruitment right.

There are lots of EQ tests online to show you your starting point and give your leader/manager candidates their starting point, too. There are also some exceptional training companies out there offering courses. Travis Bradbury's company TalentSmart (TalentSmartEQ.com) is a good example.

Turnover costs can be as high as 150–200 percent of an employee's salary.[17] Whether you're paying an entry-level

---

[15] Randall J. Beck and Jim Harter, "Why Great Managers Are So Rare," Gallup Workplace, October 30, 2024, https://www.gallup.com/workplace/231593/why-great-managers-rare.aspx.

[16] Jackie Wiles, "Great Resignation or Not, Money Won't Fix All Your Talent Problems," Gartner, December 9, 2021, https://www.gartner.com/en/articles/great-resignation-or-not-money-won-t-fix-all-your-talent-problems.

[17] Genevieve Michaels, "The True Costs of Employee Turnover," 15Five, accessed September 23, 2024, https://www.15five.com/blog/true-costs-of-turnover.

wage or a managerial salary, that's far too much money to leave on the table. And leave it you will, if you hire or promote the wrong manager or fail to develop the right skills in the ones you choose.

Don't lose staff, productivity, or customers because you have hired the wrong manager. You need managers who acknowledge the high returns on professional development and invest time, effort, and money in their people (and themselves).

Chapter 5

Leadership Styles

Every great manager brings their own personality, strengths, background, and quirks to the table, and that's what makes management such a fascinating art. The same is true of leaders. Leadership isn't a one-size-fits-all role. The key is understanding your natural tendencies, what might trip you up, and where you have room to grow.

Let's examine some common leadership styles and some circumstances where the style might be best suited (and when it fails). Once you know your starting point, you will be better able to try a different style when it is suitable, as well as know how you might level up your leadership style.

The Transactional Leader: The Taskmaster

Transactional leaders love order. They love it when deadlines are met, processes are followed, and everything runs like a well-oiled machine under their watch.

If you're the type who thrives on schedules, structure, and systems, this might be the primary style that describes you. Your team always knows what's expected, and in fast-paced, systems-strong environments, that kind of clarity is golden.

There's a risk to this style, which is that you focus more on the task at hand than on the people performing it. If your team starts to feel like robots and they're just ticking boxes for you, you might notice their energy and engagement slipping. After all, no one wants to feel like a cog in the machine.

If you're a taskmaster at heart, try shedding this style on occasion. Add a human touch to your leadership. Hit everyone's pause button during a race to the deadline in order to check in with your team's energy levels and find out what they need from you. It can make all the difference to your team's performance.

The Autocratic Leader: The Decider

Autocratic leaders are most at ease taking charge. They won't hesitate to make snap decisions while expecting their teams to follow through without discussion.

In high-pressure environments like healthcare or manufacturing, primarily using this leadership style can save time and prevent errors, especially when safety is on the line. But there's a fine line between being decisive and being overbearing.

There is always that leader who changes processes without explanation or feedback. Employees might follow orders, but they'll likely feel frustrated and disengaged.

If you lean toward an autocratic style, consider stepping away from that "My way or the highway" style for a moment to tell your team the "why" behind your decisions. Explaining your reasoning doesn't just help employees understand, it builds trust and buy-in, even when there's no room for debate.

The Consensus Leader: The Collaborator

Consensus leaders are all about collaboration and are most at ease when they include everyone on the team in the discussions and decision-making.

This leader holds team meetings where everyone's input is encouraged, from the most experienced employees to the newest hires.

This approach can build trust and ensure everyone feels heard. However, it can also slow things down when the leader just can't decide. When too many ideas and opinions are expressed and the leader is torn on the direction to take, employees might feel frustrated when things don't move forward.

If this sounds like you, balance listening with your unequivocal clear decision. For instance, you might say,

"Hey, everyone, your ideas have made all our options clear to me. We're going with Plan C—right away."

You are the leader taking responsibility for decision-making while acknowledging the input you've received. It keeps your team engaged without alienating them.

A Tale of Two Leaders #1

I have suggested that a leader needs to be aware when a change in style is required. While I'm convinced that most leaders know intuitively how to do this, let me share a manufacturing story to illustrate.

An autocratic leader had just retired from a factory position. His twelve-man team inherited a newbie leader. No surprise: Everyone was on alert at how the new guy would work out.

The newbie took the transactional approach on day one saying essentially, "Men, let's fill that quota." And he spent the whole day observing how they did so.

On day two, the newbie continued observations, and two or three times during that day made several no-discussion decisions when the men came to him for this or that. He applied the autocratic leadership approach.

On day three, however, he shocked this team of laborers. He called them all into the break room and said, "Okay, guys, talk to me. Why the bottleneck when you are transferring the finished product?"

All eyes went on alert. And finally, the dam broke. All of the men started speaking at once, even as shocked as they were at being given the opportunity! Enter the consensus leadership approach.

The team's outgoing leader had refused outright to request the replacement or repair of a piece of lifting/moving equipment that would have moved each of the completed parts down a narrow passageway on an overhead rail. He had insisted that the men manhandle the several-hundred-pound pieces down the all-too-narrow aisle to the shipping bay manually. First of all, the weight of each part took four of them to maneuver. Second of all, there was no way the aisle was safely wide enough for the four of them plus the part. Third, it was a slow, slow process. They did their best.

The new leader saw multiple workers' comp claims ready to happen if he didn't resolve this issue. So, he just asked the men, "How do you want to fix this?" As it happened, they were ready with the solution! They had a cheaper and much more satisfying, safely efficient resolution to the whole issue—it was just that no one had ever asked them for it! It took the enthusiastic team three minutes to explain it to the new guy. Then it took them all, united and working together, exactly eighty minutes to implement their solution in a permanent manner with the new leader's blessing.

Not only was the team now much safer on the job than since the breakdown of the overhead lift, but they would also have followed their new leader to the ends of the earth.

The Transformational Leader: The Visionary

That story leads me to the fourth type of leader, and as you might guess, it is a style of leadership I believe every business needs more of.

Transformational leaders are the visionaries. They are the ones who inspire their teams to think big, be creative, and push boundaries—to change and transform not only the business or the industry but each of the people within it. These leaders prioritize people and build trust by connecting with them through empathy and emotional intelligence.

They don't just focus on today's to-do list; they're looking at how today's efforts build a stronger tomorrow. It is very likely going to be this leader who sits down with employees one by one to discuss career goals, helping them see how their current role is a stepping stone to something greater.

These are the leaders who champion continuous learning. They create the budget, but also the learning plan to help their people progress and thrive because that is how the business will prosper, too.

If this resonates with you, ask yourself if you are spending enough time being present with your team. Small actions, like recognizing successes and hard work, can reinforce the culture or care that transformational leaders are known for.

What's Your Leadership Game?

Leadership isn't about being perfect; it's about learning and adapting. If you're not naturally the type of leader who recognizes the strengths and contributions of others, it's a skill and you can learn it. Like any skill, leadership requires focus, practice, experimentation, and a willingness to adapt.

Leaders across all industries and workplaces have made transformative changes in their leadership styles. You can, too. It starts with a little self-awareness. Three steps help get the ball rolling:

1. Decide which leadership style is your go-to. Start observing how it works or not in a range of situations (and keep notes!). Observe whether you intuitively shift for a moment to another more effective style or not.

2. Determine whether you fully understand your team's skills, and if you value what they all bring to the table (and then write some ways you are in fact doing that—or starting to do that).

3. Ask if you are giving your team the encouragement and resources to thrive (then write some ways you've achieved that).

Most of us need to observe our starting point before attempting any kind of change or improvement.

I've spoken about great managers and leaders who proactively identify their individual employees' strengths. The truth is that great leaders don't rely only on their own skills to get work done. They leverage the strengths of those around them. They know when to lead from the front and when to step back and let others shine.

While we are tempted to believe we have to have all the answers, make all the decisions, and carry the weight of every problem, it is also stressful and futile! Leadership isn't a solo performance under the spotlight. It's a team sport where your role is to bring out the best in everyone.

One of the biggest hurdles in leadership is learning to put your ego in check. Have you been letting your ego run the show? There will always be a manager somewhere who barks out orders and waves his arms around when the going gets tough. That's ego telling him, "Not *your* job here. You are *the boss*. Make the others catch up, make it right, do that task, race against the clock..."

You hired for talent and skills (you did, didn't you?) so let them apply their strengths to the tasks at hand. This is about trusting your team as you dial back the need to control everything. Leadership isn't static but a game of continuous adaptation. That's why experimenting with different styles is so important. You are decisive as needed; you are collaborative when the team probably has the answer or needs to know the reasons behind circumstances; you are transformative when the team needs to expand and learn, and so on.

The goal isn't to reinvent yourself as a different kind of leader for the long term but to expand your toolkit. As you try new styles, pay attention to what resonates with your team, gets the job done, and aligns with your values. Leadership is about finding the balance that works for you and the people you're leading.

How to Level Up Your Leadership Style

You will be faced with leadership challenges. It comes with the territory. As opportunities arise, try some adaptations to your own style, and as they work, add them to your toolkit.

1. **Check in:** Talk to your team and peers about how they perceive your leadership. This could be formalized as a 360-type leadership review. This is a particularly effective way to start understanding the issues when teams or businesses are struggling.

2. **Identify strengths but never stop learning:** What are you great at, and where do you need to bow to another person's knowledge based on how past decisions worked out or did not? This self-awareness is step one for anyone on a path of change or learning.

3. **Stand on the shoulders of the great ones:** Observe leaders you admire, whether living or historic. Which of their approaches can you incorporate into your style?

4. **Make small changes:** What one small change today can level up your leadership?

Leadership isn't about practicing just one style of leadership. It's about self-awareness, adaptability, situational awareness, and growing an arsenal of tools to resolve any issue that arises.

Know Your People and Their Roles

Most leaders and a fair number of managers never discuss their staff's job descriptions and compare them to the actual work done. Show up. Do this analysis. Change the job descriptions to match the job they're performing. Update the processes each one uses when your employee is doing it more efficiently than the manual. Find out what tools and resources they use or still need to perform those jobs.

You don't have to know their jobs inside and out, but you need to have a basic idea of what people are going through to get the work done. If you're in a manufacturing plant, get on the floor and talk with your operators. Learn with staff how to rotate food and follow sanitary food handling rules if you're in the food industry. Get a sense of every job performed under your purview.

Remember Where You Came From

Leaders and managers would do well to "remember their origins." By this, I mean you should write a summary of when you started your first job and map out the whole timeline and experience of that job.

We do this exercise with our clients so that people who have become leaders don't forget where they started. At nine years of age, one took on a paper route, getting up bleary-eyed at 4:30 a.m. and hopping on his bike in the cold Midwestern winter. So many executives were dishwashers with suds up to their elbows. Many were summer laborers on a construction crew. Write down the job. Write about what you learned, what you loved and disliked, what you didn't understand, and how much you were paid.

Successful leaders repeat this simple truth to themselves, "I'm not above anyone, and I'm not better than anyone. I don't expect my team to do anything I would not. I've been fortunate to step into this role, and now I have the opportunity to make a real difference in people's lives." When you focus on that, the rewards follow. Days go more smoothly and efficiently.

Motivate, Praise, Train

The job of all leaders is to connect with their people. A successful leader is filling the airways with good news. This leader is in tune with their people, asking questions when things look like they're going wrong or just differently from most days. There is support from this type of leader, and the internal customers know it.

Think about the kinds of things you do (or fail to do) to motivate, train or support, praise, and encourage your internal customers. You might be the type of leader who forgets to make that connection with your people because you're always looking at the things that went wrong. Spend your first hours every day looking at what went right and go talk to those who achieved it! Success, as they say, leaves clues.

Permission to Make Mistakes

The leaders people love to work for are humble enough to admit that they don't have every answer, and are wise enough to lean on their team's expertise and on their ability to learn. These leaders allow their people to make mistakes, and instead of playing the blame game when they occur, they use those mistakes as teaching opportunities to learn and grow together. No doubt about it: People make mistakes. It's human nature. But in the right environment, those mistakes become stepping stones for learning and growth, not punishable offenses.

Under this kind of leadership, all your internal customers thrive, perform, and seek improvement. They can take risks, make mistakes, and know they'll be supported rather than sanctioned. This mistakes-allowed, learning-encouraged approach is also where leadership has created a culture where high standards guide the way, but those standards don't become a rigid, unforgiving rule book.

The benefits of this leadership style ripple outward. When you create a culture of trust and empowerment for your internal customers, your external customers will feel it, too. It's all connected. Do right by your people, and they'll pass that energy along, building relationships and delivering experiences that reflect the strength of your leadership.

Transformational leaders are masters at balancing high expectations with empathy. They hold every employee and themselves to the same uncompromising standards, ensuring that everyone rises to the occasion. These leaders know that cutting corners isn't just a bad habit; it sets a tone that will unfortunately ripple through the organization. When you let things slide, others will follow suit. But when you lead with integrity and focus, the entire team levels up. Your people profit, your company profits, and your external customers get real value.

The Role of Standards in Leadership

Every business operates in some obvious or subtle way on standards. Often the industry is regulated, and that establishes standards of sanitation, safety and so on.

Standards are also one or more sets of internally decided expectations. They act like a GPS for your team, pointing the way forward and keeping everyone moving in the same direction and to a shared goal. Ideally (just like our vehicle's GPS) when an obstacle occurs on our route, we are offered a "detour"—an alternative path to still get to the end goal. Without standards, it's easy for processes and procedures ("standards" in their own right), and any number of isolated tasks to drift off course.

Setting standards alone is not enough. How you uphold them is what truly defines your leadership style. Here is my take on how each style of leader upholds standards:

- **Transformational Leaders** don't just enforce but model standards. They walk them and talk them and thus indirectly inspire their teams to rise to the challenge. They're the ones saying, "Here's where we're going, and I'm right here with you." These leaders hold the big strategic end goal in mind and share it, thereby creating a vision that motivates everyone to strive for excellence.

- **Transactional Leaders** excel at creating systems and processes that ensure standards are met consistently. While they may focus more on tasks and procedural matters than on people, their structure can be an invaluable standard for maintaining quality and efficiency.

- **Consensus Leaders** believe it is essential to bring the team into the conversation, using standards as a shared goal rather than a directive. By encouraging dialog, consensus leaders can create in their internal customers a real sense of "owning the outcome." That is what drives employees' commitment to the high standards you've set.

- **Autocratic Leaders** might enforce standards with precision, ensuring rules are exactly obeyed. While this can be effective in critical situations or in a highly regulated industry activity, these leaders will also benefit from balancing that authority with flexibility (that GPS alternate route) to avoid stifling creativity.

Surrounding Yourself with Excellence

My favorite leaders ascribe to the belief that "I'm not the smartest one in the room, so I have to find them and bring them in."

They cannot know it all. They acknowledge that and they build smart teams. Transformational leaders are particularly open to surrounding themselves with people who are smarter, more skilled, or more experienced in specific areas. They know that a team of all-stars beats a solo act every time.

Please note that this last isn't just a transformational leader trait—it's a hallmark of effective leadership in general. Whether you're a consensus builder or a taskmaster, the ability to identify and lean on others' strengths is crucial. Leaders who embrace this approach exude confidence, humility, and possess a deep understanding of how to get the best from their people.

The Domino Effect of High Standards

Upholding high standards isn't about perfection as many might believe, but about the *relentless pursuit* of excellence. Your standards have set the bar. Then it's about creating an expectation of accountability, learning, and quality experience for both internal and external customers. You create a culture where everyone's strengths are deployed, including your own.

When you are the first one to model those standards, your team takes notice. They see the value in doing things the right way, even when it's perhaps initially harder. That mindset doesn't just work within the team but bleeds over to your external customers.

Portrait of a Bad Leader

As you have read about the four styles of leadership, any combination of leadership styles might suit you at various junctures. The style you apply will depend on the context of the problem you are addressing but also your industry, specific activity, product or service. Knowing which style suits the circumstances is the hallmark of a good leader.

Poor leadership, on the other hand, is one big reason your internal customers flee.

Many leaders hide. They go right to their office and stay at their desk all day long. Other leaders just never help;

they never roll up their sleeves and go shoulder-to-shoulder with their staff. They're perfectly capable of dealing with an unhappy customer or taking care of something that's not in their job description. But they don't.

Disengaged leaders not only don't move the mission of the business forward, but they can also in turn make people feel so disengaged that effectiveness evaporates. They often diminish people's contributions to the organization and get under people's skin with their behavior, words, and approach. This makes your internal customer feel unheard and "less than." And through an invisible ripple effect, your clients will feel it, too. You've become a "bad leader", and such a person can create a very toxic work environment.

That quiet domino effect is operational whether you are a good or a bad leader. The effect of poor leadership ripples out to all internal customers, which results in their poor treatment of external customers, which leads external customers to post bad reviews, resulting in the business experiencing reduced sales and revenues, while turnover increases. As the last falling domino, your bottom-line profits shrivel.

A Tale of Two Leaders #2

Chili's and Marriott were two early experiences that shaped my first encounters in management, exposing me to both inspiring and toxic leadership. I quickly learned that part of the role of great leaders is to mentor their people. What many toxic leaders fail to realize, though, is that negative mentorship is also a form of mentoring, whether they intend it or not.

I had the opportunity to learn from both types of leaders. Positive mentors demonstrated to me how to work, lead, learn, and grow in the work. Positive mentors help people grow and develop their skills. Negative mentors did two things as I worked under a few of them: They demonstrate exactly how *not* to lead, and they drive talented people out of a company, no matter how much those employees love their work.

Marriott was a company I loved working for. I was in their healthcare division, working in acute care hospitals. It was one of the best experiences of my early career.

After a successful stint on the East Coast, I was transferred to a new location in California, a move that aligned perfectly with my dream of living on the West Coast. At the time, I wasn't trying to climb the corporate ladder—my goals were simpler. I envisioned working hard, enjoying life at the beach, and spending time exploring the area. I was only twenty-four years old, and that was all I wanted.

My dedication to my work, however, was unmistakable. I brought creativity to my role in healthcare, feeding doctors and nurses, and found ways to innovate within the hospital cafeteria setting that we were contracted to manage. I developed theme days that earned praise from the area director, who openly commended my efforts in front of my new general manager. But while the director was impressed, my immediate supervisor was not.

This new general manager, who hadn't been consulted about my transfer, responded with a mix of indifference and passive-aggressive behavior. She would ignore the team for days and then emerge to criticize my work, often in the harshest terms. Despite my creativity and work ethic, she made me feel inadequate on a daily basis. It soon became clear that she couldn't stand having any successful individuals around her. Her constant criticism wore me down, and within six months, I left Marriott—a company I had hoped to stay with for many years.

My experience at Chili's was vastly different. I had worked in restaurants throughout college but had never managed one. My new general manager (GM) at Chili's was a stark contrast to my Marriott manager. She was a positive mentor who encouraged creativity and independence. She not only gave me freedom to motivate the team my way but also took the time to teach me the administrative side of the business—everything from managing inventory to understanding profit and loss (P&L) statements. She knew I aspired to be a GM one day, and she actively supported me as I learned the requisite skills.

Under her mentorship, I quickly moved up to assistant GM and continued to develop both my skills and my confidence. This positive mentorship gave me the tools I needed to succeed in leadership development that could have been stifled under the wrong guidance.

I learned valuable lessons from my positive and negative mentors. I learned how to lead and how not to lead.

When I eventually transferred back to Boston, I rejoined Marriott and returned to work under the guidance of my former, supportive manager, proving that the right leadership makes all the difference.

People Profit

Does the wrong manager, supervisor, or foreman cause resignations? Definitely. Studies have found 82 percent of workers across ten industries say they would quit their jobs due to their leader's poor behavior, including a lack of openness or honesty, micromanaging, and disrespect of personal time.[18] They've also found 57 percent of employees have left a job because of their manager, while 14 percent have left multiple jobs because of them.[19]

Company leadership has an even stronger effect on employee retention than direct managers. Employees say 28 percent of their intent to stay is driven by the leadership of the business as a whole, while 12 percent is driven by direct managers. As I noted in Chapter 3, career development opportunities are the biggest factor in retention, accounting for 52 percent of employees' intent to stay.[20]

It's leadership that sets the tone, the pace, and the motivation to develop its internal customer—and that is why finding and developing an arsenal of great leadership styles will pay such great dividends.

---

18 Sara Korolevich, "Horrible Bosses: Are American Workers Quitting Their Jobs Or Quitting Their Managers?," GoodHire, January 11, 2022, https://www.goodhire.com/press-releases/warning-to-managers-survey-shows-most-workers-will-quit-a-bad-boss.
19 "New DDI Research: 57 Percent of Employees Quit Because of Their Boss," PRNewswire, December 9, 2019, https://www.prnewswire.com/news-releases/new-ddi-research-57-percent-of-employees-quit-because-of-their-boss-300971506.html.
20 Didier Elzinga, "The Biggest Lie in HR: People Quit Bosses Not Companies," Culture Amp, August 7, 2024, https://www.cultureamp.com/blog/biggest-lie-people-quit-bosses.

Chapter 6

Your External Customer and Your Market Reputation

In the last few chapters, we've explored aspects of your internal customer service. The people working behind the scenes to move your business forward include all staff, managers, and leaders.

But now, I'd like to shift the focus to your external customers and the reputation of your business in the marketplace.

Let me clarify that your external customers go beyond your population of buyers. They include vendors, suppliers, financiers, affiliates, and other external partners who support your operations. In fact, your external customer network is probably going to be more expansive than you realize. But for now, let's keep the focus narrow and look only at your buyers—the ones paying you money for your products or services.

External customers don't just come for the product. Those days are gone! Today, they come for the overall experience which encompasses not just what they buy from you, but how easy it was to complete a purchase, and how you interacted with and treated them as they did so.

Think about this "experience" in terms of the expectations they bring with them. Certainly today, customers expect lots of product/service information, a seamless buying process, and a fast turnaround once they've clicked "Buy" or walked into your business. Beyond the ease, what else do they seek? Is it personalization, a touch of luxury, stellar after-sales service? The more you understand their needs and expectations, the better equipped you are to meet and exceed them.

Customer Personas

In spite of all the data, metrics, and tools out there to measure such things, understanding your external customers is about more than just knowing demographics of 80 percent of your buyers, or gathering a running list of their buying habits.

Too many companies try to be all things to all external customers, and they end up not being very good at anything. Others don't try at all and likewise fall flat. Without a clear view of the type of business you're in, you'll never repeatedly attract the specific type of client you're looking for.

Let's take a step back and ask a deceptively simple question: *What are you really selling?*

In the food business, we certainly expect that what is on the plate and who we interact with to receive it is the basic formula for any restaurant. If, however, you're in fine dining, diners might also be seeking the romance, elegance, and ambiance that transforms an ordinary meal into a memorable experience. The meal becomes a special event, a memorable story to tell later.

In the professions or any service business, you might be transactional in the knowledge or skill you sell. The plumber and the attorney are each selling specific knowledge, yes, but also a convenient, relief-filled solution to most of their external customers.

A *Customer Persona* is a description of your ideal or typical customer—the person you're specifically targeting. Don't confuse this description with demographic profiling, which is more data driven. A customer persona is behavioral. It aims to determine the personal interests, motivations, and preferences of specific individuals or narrow groups of like individuals rather than your total target population of buyers.

Picture yourself on the floor of a busy car dealership and as you do, remember that customers come in with distinct personas, unique needs, and expectations that are impossible to guess by looking at the person. You'll find it necessary to gather information, build something of a relationship, and get context ... before you even start to show cars to your buyers.

For instance, you might encounter:

1. Two parents with young children, shopping for a family car that balances safety, reliability, and plenty of cargo space for all those weekend soccer games, and grocery runs.

2. An older teen or college student with a proud parent, ready to buy their first car as a gift for graduation or a send-off to new adventures. Their excitement is palpable, but so is the parent's focus on economy, practicality, and purchase price.

3. A single, mid-thirties, well-dressed woman, looking for a full-sized sedan that reflects her professionalism while providing comfort and performance for her daily commute and occasional road trips.

Each of these customers has a different story, and your goal as a sales professional for the dealership is to uncover it. You will fail utterly if you don't learn their story and simply try to sell the exact same car to each one of them.

This is where relationship selling comes into play. Instead of diving straight into showing vehicles, you take the time to talk to them, ask questions, and truly listen. By asking questions, you're not just gathering information. You're building trust. Customers want to feel like you're genuinely invested in finding the right solution for them, not just closing the deal. It's about helping them find the car that fits their life.

This approach shifts the focus from a transactional exchange to a meaningful interaction. And when you connect with them on this level, you're not just selling a car. You're creating an experience they'll remember and talk about long after they drive off the lot.

That leads me to a golden rule to live by that assists us all in creating that first connection: Ask, don't assume. Listen, don't speak.

Making assumptions about your customers can cost you—big time. It's tempting to size someone up as they walk through the door, but appearances can be deceiving and getting it wrong could mean watching them take their business elsewhere.

Consider a car dealership scenario: A father and daughter stroll into a car dealership, dressed in their comfy weekend clothes, maybe a little scruffy and wind-blown after a day of errands and chores. The salesperson assumes they're just browsing, not serious buyers, and leaves them to their own devices in the showroom without approaching them.

What didn't the salesperson know? That the father and daughter had the cash ready to pay for a car *on the spot*.

That they were looking at two specific models for sale in the showroom. That they wanted to close on a deal *today*.

Why didn't the salesperson know this? He never approached or spoke to them! Instead, these potential buyers walked right out the door and made their purchase at a dealership down the street where a salesperson actually paid attention to them the instant they walked in.

The first salesperson didn't even attempt to create a relationship. Don't be fooled: Asking three questions would have started "a relationship" but he didn't do it. The second salesperson clearly not only opened a relationship with a "Welcome to our showroom! Come on in, I'm Jasper," but kept on asking questions and building it until he knew exactly what to present to his now-known customer. He'd uncovered a quick but accurate customer persona in just a few short minutes with a few questions.

Asking questions isn't just polite. It's strategic. It's relationship-building. It establishes expectations so that you can meet them (or become sure you cannot). It shows your customers that you're genuinely interested in their needs and willing to inform and guide them, not just sell to them.

Curiosity creates connection, and connection builds trust. When you take the time to ask, "What are you looking for?" or "What brings you in today?" you open the door to understanding and meeting their expectations. The lesson here? Don't let assumptions write the narrative for you. Let your curiosity do the work instead.

Shape Expectations Proactively

The point is that no matter what your industry, what you're selling is more than meets the eye. It's not just about the "what." The "what" is about features. Your product has a "what." It comes in twelve colors. Even a service has a "what." You sell a professionally drafted Last Will and Testament. Those are features.

What you are selling (and that you succeed in selling it) is much more about the "why." The "why" is the benefits of your product as perceived by the buyer. Your product is easier to operate than all competing ones—thank goodness! Your skillful, timely service call and repair prevents their whole basement from flooding—relief! Those are benefits to someone buying convenience and resolutions.

The more you understand the deeper value and benefits behind what you offer, the better you'll identify their customer persona and be able to meet expectations and communicate value to your customers. And when customers see the benefits behind what you know, do, and sell, they're far more likely to stick with you, recommend you, and see you as an indispensable part of their lives.

Shape the story you tell the world—the expectations of your external customers—by considering your product or service from the buyers' perspective but also by how you differentiate yourself from others in your industry.

I know of a small business that does crime and trauma scene cleaning. "Cleaning" is "what" they do. Imagine for a moment how they best communicate what business they are actually in, to which target market, and the buyer benefits of hiring them. I guarantee their message differs from that of the Molly Maids residential cleaning service down the road! Their "what" might both be expressed as "cleaning"—but their "why" is totally different.

In every business, no matter what you sell or who you sell it to, understanding your customers' personas is essential. Why? Knowing what is motivating their decision to buy, as well as knowing how to communicate effectively with them, is what allows you to create a great customer experience. But this isn't just about collecting data—it's about forming a relationship (however brief). Teach staff to listen, pick up on cues, and connect with the people they serve, because when your team knows how to engage with customers on a deeper level, everyone wins.

Your Reputation in the Market

I addressed this briefly in Chapter 2 when I suggested you could find out more about your company's reputation with internal customers through Glassdoor reviews.

This, however, is a bit more about your external customers. Why are some customers so challenging to deal with? It's a question every business has wrestled with at some point. From what I've observed, it often comes down to one underlying issue: a lack of trust that you can fulfill expectations. Many customers walk into businesses already braced for disappointment. They've been let down too many times by poor service, empty promises, or halfhearted efforts. It's the climate of skepticism that has become all too common.

How many times have you, as a customer, felt like you weren't being told the whole truth about a product or about the final price of a service? This sense of distrust makes customers more defensive, more demanding, and, yes, more difficult. And unfortunately, it's a vicious cycle—low expectations lead to disengagement by businesses, which only reinforces the cynicism.

You and your team have a job: It's about recognizing the full scope of the external customers' expectations (and your ability to meet them), the value they bring to your business, and the reputation you're building with every interaction.

Your external relationships are part of a much bigger story that connects your team, your values, and your vision for the future.

1. Do you know what your external customers value most about your business? *How* do you know?

2. What are they telling others about their experience with you? *How* do you know?
    a. If it is bad news, what are you doing to correct the issue?
    b. If it is good news, what are you doing to perpetuate it?

Want to really understand your external customers? Start by talking to your internal customers. Yes, we are back to them, and you shouldn't be surprised! They're the ones on the front lines—whether face-to-face, at a keyboard, or behind the wheel. They're taking calls, handling returns, managing deliveries, and interacting with customers every single day. In short, they've got the inside scoop on what's working, what's not, and what your customers are really saying.

As a leader aiming to stand out, innovate, and make a lasting impact, you need to keep your ear to the ground. Listening to your team isn't just a box to check—it's a golden opportunity to uncover insights and make continuous improvements.

When you ask for input, however, don't let it devolve into a gripe-fest. Sure, frustrations will surface, but that's not where the conversation ends—it's where it begins. Take those gripes and turn them into opportunities for brainstorming. What changes could you make to resolve those pain points and boost customer satisfaction? Could a better tracking tool streamline a clunky process? Would tweaking a procedure make things smoother for both employees and customers?

The point is to listen, act, and create solutions that not only improve customer experience but also make life easier for your team. Because when your internal customers feel supported and empowered, your external customers will notice—and love it.

So many companies—of all sizes and in all industries—are doing just enough to get by. They allow themselves to be mediocre. One negative review goes viral in seconds, while a good review is ignored. If you're getting all five-star rave reviews, people don't believe it and do proactive deep dives to find the more negative reviews, which have come to be seen as "the real ones." Needless to say, too many negative reviews and not enough five-star ones can destroy your business.

Knowing those answers will help you make decisions to strengthen all of your external relationships to create even greater value on both sides. Your external customers should represent more to you and your staff than just transactions. They're partners in your success and expect to be treated as such.

You have the power to break the cycle of low expectations. You do it by delivering *"unexpectedly excellent"* service. This is service that exceeds what customers imagined was even possible. When you wow a customer, you're doing more than solving their immediate problem—you're changing their perception. You differentiate your business from "those other ones." And here's the magic: When you gain their trust, the "difficult" exterior often melts away. Trust opens the door to cooperation, understanding, and loyalty.

Market Reputation: The Silent Salesperson

Your business has a reputation, and whether you've actively shaped it or not, it's out there, telling your story to your buyers who are—never forget—looking for an experience that meets or exceeds their expectations. That story is your reputation and is the narrative that spreads through the marketplace coloring how every single outsider perceives you.

But here's the rub: Reputations aren't always what you think they are. We forget that they are shaped by all our customers—the internal ones and the external ones!

Reputations are reshaped by every interaction, every personal conversation, every online review, every moment of truth when a customer or partner engages with your business.

You don't want a "default" story out there. You want to choose and craft your reputation, your brand story.

Knowing the story (the default or the crafted) that's out there about your business helps you know why people choose you over your competitors—or have fled to your competitors after one purchase from you. You must know what it is about your product, your team, or your process that makes them say, "This is where I'll buy!" If they're not choosing you, why not? This is critical information to possess, and it can unlock valuable insights into your business.

And that brings us back to internal customer service . . .

A New Standard

The bar is so often set low by your competition when it comes to external and internal customer service, that you have a golden opportunity. Exceeding expectations doesn't have to be about grand gestures. Sometimes, it's as simple as starting to implement one new relationship-building action (actively listening, being transparent about options, or going just a little out of your way to create convenience for the customer) and building from there with more such actions. In the face of your competition, your customer may allow such small moments to build some trust for you. When you can repeat the experience and then systematize it, this new trust is what transforms a difficult customer into a loyal one and sets your business apart in their minds.

Marketing and Branding

The other thing that speaks loudly to your external customers is your marketing messages and your clearly devised brand. State the problem you're solving in your messaging, so people know you're their go-to resource. Then follow through and keep your promises with each external customer. You have to—you told them you would. If you don't, your brand (your business reputation) takes a hit.

When I owned my fitness center, one of the things I hammered into our staff was to clean the bathrooms every half hour. They made sure to pick up guest towels and wipe down all surfaces, and they vacuumed the locker rooms every three hours.

Does that seem excessive to you? One type of review that came in many different times was statements about how clean our fitness center was and how comfortable people felt in that environment. That's part of how our membership grew from eighty-eight members to six hundred in a seven-year period. It was because of our reputation as a brand. We had name recognition and an excellent reputation for cleanliness, which instantly expanded to never allowing sweat-covered equipment. None of our staff wanted to see a single drop of sweat on the pads or bars. We never left trash or linens lying around, no matter how neglectful our customers might have been. We took pride in our workplace and the atmosphere we created, and it paid off.

As I talked about in the last chapter, once you've set those high standards, you need to make them nonnegotiable. I understood that our clientele at the fitness center were first and foremost, upper-market people. They paid not to have a bullpen type of national franchise club to exercise. Our customers wanted the experience of working out in a place that was clean, where they knew the staff cared about who they were and what their goals might be. We used members' names from the moment they signed up and every time they came in. We asked and cared about their overall health and wellness.

Members would walk in, and even before scanning their check-in card (which made their name pop up on the screen), we would say, "Hey, Margaret" or "Hey, Joe," plus another personalized comment that we knew was appropriate. We would ask, "Hey, Jenn, tell us about that new event you're working out for." Or a new member would hear, "What are your goals?" We also knew when people were getting married soon ("Congrats! Do you have goals you want to achieve before the wedding?") and so on. We got involved in their fitness and their club experience, and we knew them. We formed groups to do warrior dashes or run marathons. Would there be only five or six of us running a 5K or 10K marathon? Yes. But the word got out, and the interest grew. It became a community. We had nothing like the big-box gym's anonymous in-and-out atmosphere—we were on another planet.

Our nickname was Cheers Without the Beer. *Cheers* is an old TV show set in a downstairs bar "where everybody knows your name." That was our fitness center. Part of the nickname came from the fact that our gym was not a storefront with street visibility. We were on the lower level of a hotel with no windows and no visibility (sort of like the TV bar). The other reason for the nickname was that we really did know every member's name!

What we did have was strong word-of-mouth referrals and community buzz. We created an experience and built relationships with members that led them to refer others to our business, because the level of service was built on a dual foundation of high standards and a deep understanding of our customers. Through my staff's genuine interest and love of the people and the work, we grew from eighty-eight to six hundred members in seven years.

Our fitness club had competition all around us. But the community of members we engaged with didn't want those options. They wanted us because of the experience we offered them at every single visit. And in the process, our top and bottom lines benefited from the holistic, transactional-plus-relational approach.

Engage/Disengage

Once you've identified your customers' personas and understand their motivations, you need to ensure that your internal customers are delivering the experience those customers expect and deserve.

Knowing how your customers perceive their interaction with your business is essential. It's the first step to addressing any internal issues that might be affecting them. Let's face it. Sometimes your internal customers just have moments of overwhelm or frustration. You might hear things like, "Why can't these shoppers just stay home? We've been swamped!"

While that sentiment might feel relatable in the heat of the moment, it's actually a good problem to have. The alternative? No shoppers at all, and no revenue coming in.

If your employees are disengaged—if they're giving off that "Me? I'm just here to punch a clock" vibe in front of every customer, how are your customers going to react to that? Imagine calling a business for help, and the person answering sighs audibly into the mike before saying, "Hello, this is Davy, how can I help?" Do you feel important to the business at that moment? Of course not.

That energy is contagious, and not in a good way.

The worst part for both customers and business? That interaction sticks with the customers. It shapes how they think about the business as a whole. Your reputation just got flushed out to sea by one more customer for whom you did not create the expected buying experience. We can all name one or more businesses where the external customer is made to feel like an inconvenience to your internal customers. Don't be that business, or soon you'll have no business.

Address disengagement at its source. Disengaged, disempowered employees with no training or support from their leaders cannot deliver exceptional service. If you sense that certain employees are struggling or have mentally/emotionally checked out, find out why. Is it a lack of training? Are they unclear about their role? Or maybe they feel undervalued, unsupported, or overwhelmed. Whatever the issue, addressing it is critical—not just for their sake, but for your external customers.

Help your team understand external customers' personas and motivations, the need for touch points that bring value to buyers. This must not be just data or information tucked away in the marketing department or the operations manager's spreadsheet! When all staff understand the expectations of buyers (and how they are or are not meeting them), you have teaching opportunities to level up your customer experience and build a team that's fully aligned with your mission.

When your whole team understands your customers' needs and knows how to meet them, it creates alignment. Your customers feel important because they're being questioned and heard. Your employees feel empowered because they know how to make a difference and find solutions for customers. And you, as the leader, can watch those relationships strengthen and grow.

The impact ripples outward. It's not just about knowing who your customers are—it's about creating an environment where every interaction, from the first hello to the final thank-you, reflects the values and standards of your business.

When the company doesn't perform, top-line sales stagnate, and bottom-line profits disappear. And that impacts everyone. Employees risk job security, and leaders face the hard reality of missed opportunities. But rather than letting this frustration linger and bleed into the external customer experience, it's an opportunity for leadership to step in.

As a leader, this is your wake-up call to pay attention. Take the time to address the workload, listen to your team's concerns, and find ways to support them. Whether it's adjusting processes, reallocating resources, or simply boosting morale, your intervention can make all the difference. When internal challenges are solved effectively, your employees can refocus their energy on delivering exceptional service while your external customers feel the impact in the best way possible.

Many businesses know their ebbs and flows and act accordingly. An example is the tax service during tax season. Staff expect a flood tide of taxpayers coming through the door, and they're ready for them. Yes, they're perhaps stressed out to the max, and when you walk in, you may not feel the love. However, a good tax business will make sure at least one person is there to greet every walk-in taxpayer. It won't be an accountant but an intake employee so that they have the energy and the wherewithal to create a good experience for clients despite the stress.

In this vein, a campground business knows that summer and holiday times are busiest, and the best businesses ramp up to greet every camper, keep the place extra clean, and process campers in and out quickly.

Restaurants know that Valentine's Day reservations go through the roof but still strive to create the great atmosphere the diner expects for this special meal.

In any industry you name, whatever you sell, and whatever business model you use to do it, you need to make sure you're positioned well to understand and know who your external customers are, what their expectations are, and how you are (or aren't) meeting them.

Relationship- and Trust-Building Ideas

Walmart's online ordering and home delivery services boomed during COVID and has kept up that momentum, no secret about it. One simple thing they did to stay connected to those online consumers since they couldn't chat face-to-face was to send an NPS survey email to each consumer one day after the delivery. You can be sure that when WalMart sends several million of those "Feedback please!" emails per hour or per day, it is getting huge numbers of valuable feedback from real consumers. They are staying in touch. They are building the relationship. They are preparing the next purchase by that consumer. Is it automated? Yes, and it works.

Start by showing your customers that you see them as individuals with whom you have a relationship, not just a transaction. Consider subscribing to an online card and gift service that makes personalization easy. When a new client comes into your business, add them to your database immediately. From there, set up automatic actions such as quarterly thank-you cards or simple birthday or holiday gifts. This makes it about them, not you. Likewise, periodically asking for and acting on feedback whether it is a formal NPS survey, or an informal questionnaire is a game-changer for building trust. It shows you're invested in their happiness, not just their business.

Create moments of delight to kick-start or further enhance the customer experience. For new clients, consider putting together a small welcome package—think branded notebooks, pens, or even a sample of your product. Send out a random "just because" discount to longtime customers with a note like, "We're happy you are our client and wanted to thank you with this small token of appreciation." And also, after a major purchase or service, follow up with a thank-you email or a quick call to check in. This shows you're thinking about them beyond the transaction.

Thoughtfulness is powerful, but consistency of connection is what sets businesses apart. Use tools and systems to automate caring gestures so that they happen regularly without falling through the cracks. Every business can build systems to stay consistent in their touches with customers. Use a customer relationship management system to track birthdays, anniversaries, and purchase histories, triggering personalized messages, calls, or gifts.

Even the smallest actions can create a ripple effect (or chain reaction if you prefer) that builds loyalty and strengthens relationships. The key is to start somewhere. Over time, these little actions can transform your business into one that customers rave about and recommend to everyone they know. Creating a climate of care isn't just a strategy. It's a commitment to putting your customers at the heart of everything you do.

The Power of Picking Up the Phone

I hear every day that people are burned out on texts and overwhelmed by emails. There are times when a text message or email just doesn't cut it. Some issues need more than typed words—and if you are in that kind of business or situation, you know who you are! That's how connections are made, and those connections are what drive loyalty, future referrals, and glowing reviews.

Hearing a person's actual voice changes the dynamic and makes the interaction feel more meaningful.

People Profit

There is profit to be made from the synergy between your internal and external customers, no doubt about it!

You must get to know your external customers and their personas and be more directly in touch with them throughout the buying process. You must not hide data in your departments but share with the whole internal team what your reputation in the marketplace has become and must transform into.

Through the synergistic efforts of your internal customers, getting to know their external customers and their expectations, you can proceed to what is often called *personalization*. McKinsey has gathered data about the benefits of this personalized approach, including these notable points:

- Companies that *excel* at personalization generate 40 percent more revenue from those activities than average players, regardless of industry.

- Consumers don't just want personalization, they demand it. They expect brands to demonstrate that they know them.

- Over 70 percent of consumers expect companies to deliver personalized interactions, and 76 percent get frustrated when it doesn't happen.[21]

---

21 Nidhi Arora, Daniel Ensslen, Lars Fiedler, Wei Wei Liu, Kelsey Robinson, Eli Stein, and Gustavo Schüler, "The Value of Getting Personalization Right—or Wrong—Is Multiplying," McKinsey, November 12, 2021, https://www.mckinsey.com/capabilities/growth-marketing-and-sales/our-insights/the-value-of-getting-personalization-right-or-wrong-is-multiplying.

Chapter 7

Mistakes, Recovery, and Leveling Up

Too many companies spend too many man hours correcting mistakes, whether it is a wrong order "someone" sent out to a client, a missed appointment "someone" forgot to calendar with a key client, data that "someone" entered wrong and that led to a whole series of (finally caught!) miscalculations, or a step in the process that "someone" forgot to take. Mistakes are made, and in a huff, "someone" repairs it, but only just enough to move on. No one learned anything from the mistake, so it occurs again and again.

Mistakes, while uncomfortable in the moment, are invaluable teaching opportunities for leaders who choose to embrace them. They provide a chance to improve internal customer service by turning setbacks into lessons. Transformational leaders understand that continuous improvement in the business requires a two-part process as far as mistakes are concerned: first, acknowledging that something went wrong, and second, learning from it to drive meaningful and sustainable whole-business improvement.

Mistakes Are Inevitable

First, you need to admit that mistakes are going to happen, no matter how well-intentioned and well-trained you all are. This means you need to make it safe for your staff to make but more importantly acknowledge mistakes in the first place—it's a double-edged opportunity that you are missing if you do not allow this to occur. When you foster an environment where employees are allowed to make mistakes without belittlement or shaming, you'll have a staff that feels more empowered in their work and in their skills.

I hope (as you have read this far) you see the risks you run when your internal culture is shaped by an autocratic leader and your people are afraid to not only make mistakes but also own up to any. That fear colors the vibe of your workplace. It will eventually bleed over into your external customers' experience of your business. This happens because you've created a monster: Employees aren't willing to be proactive in solving issues, taking risks, thinking outside the box, or being innovative. They perceive it as too risky.

You can't recover from or correct a mistake you refuse to acknowledge. Recovery from mistakes is a function of your internal culture and the way you handle things as a leader. We've talked about the high standards you set for yourself and your team. If an employee doesn't meet that standard and your reaction is to belittle or condescend, you've just broken their confidence and trust in themselves as well as in you. It also erodes their work ethic because they know that if they make a mistake or do anything wrong, you're the one who is going to step in and take over. They end up not caring as much anymore about the quality or importance of their work because of how you've reacted to their mistakes. They disengage and you have a downward spiral of inefficiencies.

You must model this behavior to your internal customers. If you've made a mistake, own whatever went wrong! Telling your people you goofed is more than leadership—it's a way to show your team that growth and accountability go hand in hand. This approach to your own mistakes actually makes you more relatable. Letting your team see that you're not perfect—because trust me, they already know—doesn't diminish your leadership; it enhances it. People respect leaders who take responsibility, learn from their missteps, and model resilience. They'll think, "If the boss can admit to a mistake and recover gracefully, maybe I can, too." Own your errors. It beats the alternative of everyone pretending they didn't notice. Trust me, they noticed.

With a healthy approach to mistakes, your teams become comfortable with making mistakes and try harder not to make them in the first place. They are more at ease taking risks and being innovative.

Turning Mistakes into Growth Opportunities

First is that you and everyone are encouraged to take a few calculated risks, make mistakes, and own them without fear. The second part of this two-part process is to make it a whole-team practice to use every mistake as a learning experience, as you collectively implement a plan to *improve your systems and service.*

The way to benefit across the business from mistakes is to first learn how it happened. This helps determine if a legacy process or whatever was behind the mistake needs to be updated so it doesn't happen again.

When mistakes happen, gathering the team for a debrief can be one of the most valuable exercises you'll do. It's about taking a collective, solutions-focused approach: "We've run into an issue. Let's figure out why it happened and what we can do to make sure it doesn't happen again."

A team debrief should feel collaborative and constructive (you transactional and autocratic leaders will note the need to momentarily pivot to achieve this!) because what you want is for everyone to go into learning-and-improving mode. It's a chance for everyone to step back, analyze what went wrong, and brainstorm ways to avoid similar pitfalls in the future. For example, you might ask your team to examine current processes and procedures for weaknesses, inefficiencies, or gaps. Was this always a bottleneck? What steps in our legacy processes could be streamlined or improved to avoid this happening again?

What you will start to notice as you address all mistakes in this manner is a pattern for improving your internal customer service. These updates certainly enhance the external customer experience. But more interestingly, it is the collaborative "fix and improve" energy that gets your internal customers providing better solutions, feeling a stronger sense of ownership of success, and stepping up their game in all circumstances.

Thus, debriefing isn't just about fixing what went wrong for your external customers—it's also a powerful tool for improving your internal dynamics. When you approach mistakes with emotional intelligence, you open the door to *improved internal customer service*. Taking an all-hands-on-deck collaborative, brainstorming approach is about more than problem-solving—it's about showing your team that you value their insights and are committed to creating a workplace where they can thrive, deploy and hone their skills, and own a piece of the success. Debriefs help build a culture of trust and continuous improvement. They show your team that it's okay to acknowledge missteps because those moments lead to better processes, stronger collaboration, and improved outcomes.

It's important to take this second, learn-and-improve step with your team. Allowing that mistakes are going to happen doesn't mean you allow the same ones to occur over and over. It's worth remembering that the tone you set as a leader matters, and that, as needed, you do have the skill to pivot into a different style of leadership to make it happen. Bring your curiosity rather than your judgment; your team will feel more able to share their thoughts openly. That's where this teaching moment and this debriefing to create an all-hands correction of the issue are key. Then, whenever an external customer service issue arises, you have employees who will think on their feet to come up with innovative solutions. They'll start brainstorming, alone or together, to make things right for your external customer. By encouraging everyone to own their mistakes and then turn them into teaching, learning, and improvement moments, you'll see your internal customers dare to take the initiative (because now they can) and solve a problem with innovation (when before they wouldn't).

Your external customers will come to appreciate and trust this culture of always making it right. They'll end up staying with you longer, not because you never make mistakes but because when any employee or any part of your process screws up, you admit it. You have to earn and re-earn their trust and their business. Never procrastinating and always attempting to make it right makes your customers feel they're in business with the right people.

A project management business I know of had recently gone through transitions in administrative assistants, and was struggling to train their third new admin. A few activities and appointments fell through the cracks in the process, notably a missed kickoff appointment with the PM and a new client's staff. The new admin hadn't entered the

PM's meeting date on the internal team calendar, and no one caught it till it was too late. The client was waiting for a PM who never showed up.

However, the team had this new admin's back—and the things were made right with the client right away. The PM was instantly on the phone with her client contact, explained, and booked a new appointment a few hours later. The client actually laughed, saying, "Boy, and here I thought we were the ones who made the mistake! I have a new admin as well!" A good laugh was shared and the admins in two businesses got a rush course in how to schedule appointments!

Just Solutions

How does your team currently handle mistakes? Are you prioritizing personal, direct communication during recovery moments? What steps can you take to replace blame with collaboration and growth?

Remember, it's not about avoiding mistakes entirely. I think you would agree that's a pipe dream. Instead, it's about handling them in a way that builds trust, strengthens relationships, and sets the stage for continuous improvement.

In business, blame can show up in unexpected places. Sometimes, managers blame team members for mistakes. Other times, companies shift the blame onto a supplier. Or worse, onto clients. But let's be clear: Blaming anyone, whether it's an internal or external customer, is one of the most counterproductive things you can do.

Train yourself and your team to always take a solution-focused approach. It's about building a culture of accountability and resilience. But here's an important piece of the puzzle: Recovery isn't just about the process. It's about the people.

Every mistake is a chance to connect with and strengthen your team and your operations. By fostering an environment where mistakes are met with understanding and solutions—not blame—you create a culture where people feel empowered to take responsibility and learn from missteps. That culture doesn't just benefit your internal customers—it radiates outward, enhancing the experience for your external customers as well.

Internally, you'll hopefully get to a point of trust and loyalty so that when any one of you makes a mistake, you move automatically into learning, recovering, and moving on. There's no agonizing or blowback. There's no hesitation since you've shown them the formula to apply: Own it. Analyze what needs fixing. Fix it. Communicate the fix. Move on.

One more word to autocratic and transactional leaders: Prepare for accolades from your own bosses when you apply this formula to your teams! Your teams will become more effective, more efficient, and happier to work with you than ever before and your executive management will take note and pat you on the back. Shifting leadership styles momentarily to achieve that? It's worth it and contributes to whole-business improvements.

External Customers Are Impatient

If you eat out a lot or happen to be in the food industry, you know this: There are so many choices of where to dine or grab a quick bite in even the smallest communities, that if one business disappoints you just one time—you're gone for good. There are too many other great places to eat.

More and more, with social media broadcasting negative reviews over the ether, and most people pre-shopping on the web before buying from even local businesses, businesses have to be on their toes all the time to provide an outstanding experience for them.

When it comes to external customers, time is of the essence. If something goes wrong, don't procrastinate. Don't delay. Don't schedule the fix or the customer callback for the fourth Wednesday of the month but instead act immediately. Whether it's a quick phone call or a video message embedded in an email, a sincere apology combined with a clear explanation of how you're making it right can work wonders. Then you can't wait to get the team together and implement the fix. Acting quickly shows your customers that they are important to you, and it often brings them back on board faster than you might expect.

Set the stage for continuous attention to glitches or potential glitches in your processes. Learn from each other. Implement improvements. You have, in fact, set the bar just that much higher, with everyone's buy-in. When you model this approach within your own team, before long, the entire organization sits up and takes notice and soon the whole business is operating within a culture of learning and growth. Here's the triple bonus:

1. A culture of continuous improvement *simultaneously* benefits both internal and external customers.

2. Your continuous improvement *differentiates* you from the competition and external customers take notice.

3. It boosts your *top and bottom lines*. More revenue. More profit.

Mistakes happen, but it's how you handle them that sets you apart. Recovery done right doesn't just bring customers back, it propels your business forward.

Celebrating Success

Transformational leaders seize upon teaching moments but remember they don't only arise from mistakes. Successes—those moments when everything went right—are just as valuable, if not more so for implementing improvements. They offer an incredible opportunity to analyze *what* worked, *why* it worked, and *how* to replicate it over and over again.

That's where debriefing on successes comes in. First, as with mistakes, you acknowledge that success occurred with a nod of congratulations to those involved in it, then you proceed with your team to dissect how it happened. Tell everyone: "We have to know what we did right in order to do it over and over again!"

Was it a specific approach, a creative solution, or simply stellar teamwork? Did someone "tweak" the process and . . . it worked better? If so, make it a permanent change. This success-analysis process helps you reinforce a culture of excellence and recognition.

When you acknowledge a particular success, celebrate it, then analyze it, here's what you can gain:

1. **Repeatability:** When you understand what led to that great outcome, you can create or modify a process around it and thus make it a repeatable achievement.

2. **Recognition:** Taking time to celebrate great outcomes balances with owning and fixing poor outcomes. A nod to every success shows your team that their hard work is noticed and appreciated. It boosts morale and motivates everyone to keep striving for excellence as they also start paying attention to *how* things go right or wrong!

3. **Prevention:** Successes also reveal what *could* have gone wrong but didn't. By analyzing these near misses, you can correct or change your processes and procedures.

The next time an employee knocks it out of the park in any way, use their brilliance as a model for training others, so their methods can benefit the entire team. Ask lots of questions to determine how they did it (and you might find that they themselves are not quite sure until the team helps them break it down!) and get everyone involved.

That's how you collectively raise your already-high standards so that they become attainable in a repeatable manner. These insights are pure gold for creating or improving your Standard Operating Procedures (SOPs). The goal is to capture the steps, approaches, and mindsets behind each success and make them actionable for others. This ensures that success isn't tied to just one person or one moment—it becomes part of the fabric of your organization.

WAIT: A Tool for Success

Here's a handy acronym to keep in mind: WAIT or *What Am I Thinking?* It's a reminder to dig into the brains of your most successful employees. Ask them to share their thought process, strategies, and decision-making steps. What may feel natural to them could be a game-changing insight for others. By capturing these details, you're building a playbook for success that anyone on your team can follow.

Take a moment to think about how you handle successes. Are you debriefing on wins with the same focus you bring to mistakes? How are you capturing successful practices and turning them into actionable processes? Are you celebrating and recognizing the people behind every success to inspire others?

Mistakes are not an unfortunate occurrence, and success isn't just a happy accident—each creates a teachable moment. You're not just fostering a culture of improvement—you're building a culture of excellence.

I talked about positive and negative mentors in Chapter 5. The behaviors I've discussed in this chapter related to mistakes and successes should serve as models, especially for new people coming into the organization. For those who have been in limbo, floating along in a job, whether they're slow to learn or just acting like a cog in the machine, modeling can level them up by giving them a successful template to emulate.

Leveling up occurs at each improvement. You achieve this in one team, and then the leaders of the next teams emulate your successes, followed finally by a great portion of the company's internal customers. The goal is to have everyone gently leveling up higher and higher across the organization, all the time. There's a low-key pressure on all team leads and managers to create the same kind of environment for their internal clients as for their external clients. And those who don't want to do that will weed themselves out, which helps you build a good staff, managers, and leaders that really care.

People Profit

The ROI of a staff dedicated to learning and leveling up their game in all the ways available is undeniable and multifaceted. Let's look at the benefits to a company with a learning culture that is open to examining, improving from its (and its competitors') mistakes, and leveling up as a whole business. Deloitte found that companies with a strong learning culture are:

- Ninety-two percent more likely to develop novel products and processes.

- Fifty-two percent more productive.

- Fifty-eight percent more likely to be the first to market with their products and services.

- Seventeen percent more profitable than their peers.

- Their engagement and retention rates are also thirty to 50 percent higher.[22]

A Korn/Ferry study discovered that organizations with the highest rates of "highly learning agile" executives created 25 percent higher profit margins than their competitors.[23] A

---
[22] "Becoming Irresistible: A New Model for Employee Engagement," Deloitte Insights, 2021, https://www2.deloitte.com/us/en/insights/deloitte-review/issue-16/employee-engagement-strategies.html.
[23] James L. Lewis, "Leadership That Drives Profits," Korn/Ferry Institute, May 2013, https://www.kornferry.com/content/dam/kornferry/docs/article-migration/SmartGrowthProof-Point_03.pdf

study by the American Society for Training and Development (ASTD) found that companies that invest in employee development see 218 percent higher revenue per employee than those that don't.[24]

---

[24] William J. Rothwell, *ASTD Models for Workplace Learning and Performance: Roles, Competencies, and Outputs* (American Society for Training and Development, 1998).

Chapter 8

Be the Disruptor in Your Field

Within the context of internal customer service that we have developed, there are basically two paths your business could follow to become a disruptor in your field:

1. Through an innovative, never-before-seen product, service, or delivery method.

2. Through the development of your internal customer service that is not only unique but unparalleled in your industry.

If you've been following to this point, you've probably understood that you'll only ever achieve the first by materializing the second. It's the people and the internal customer service that you develop that make everything happen. Everything.

Every business absolutely has the potential to be a disruptor. It starts with a single focus on your internal customers and the service you provide for them. You now know to start there. Simply because most businesses overlook this crucial foundation, that's where your opportunity lies. If you want to stand out, be a disruptor in your approach to internal customer service.

We are living in a remarkable time in history where a typical workforce spans several generations and possesses a variety of experiences, skills, and ways of thinking.

Some of your older employees began their careers before the tech revolution reshaped everything. They've seen industries adapt to seismic shifts and have not only grown with and adapted to the myriad changes but likely also played a key role in either developing or driving them. Many of the groundbreaking products, services, and delivery methods we take for granted today were created by individuals with decades of experience under their belts.

On the other hand, young members of the workforce grew up fully immersed in the digital age. They were born into a world where smartphones and instant connectivity weren't novelties but the norm. With a computer in every hip pocket, this group is also redefining how businesses operate, by launching and running multimillion-dollar ventures or successful side hustles straight from their kitchen tables, coffee shop booths, or even while traveling the globe.

What connects these groups within your business is a shared willingness and ability to navigate and thrive in disruption. By expecting and leading collaboration, you'll benefit from a dynamic flood of ideas—a wide range of approaches to efficiency, innovation, and problem-solving. To leaders paying attention (and riding the wave), this diverse thinking about business offers immense potential. The key is allowing every voice to be heard, and every contribution to be acknowledged. Your role as "a disruptive leader" is to encourage curiosity, make sense of the ideas arising from it, and align them with the needs, goals, and values of the business.

What Exactly Is a Disruptor?

By definition, a disruptor challenges the status quo of their industry. They look at their traditional SOPs and look beyond their industry to how others do it all better. They know that if they have a problem in business, someone in the world has already solved it, and seek out that solution.

There is simply no call to be the "best in town" when you can reach out and be the "best in the world." Whether it's adapting to new AI tools; rethinking legacy processes; or doing things "the way that company halfway around the world does it" because it is simply more effective ... disruption can easily become your norm.

Disruptors aren't afraid to reach out (and yes, even halfway around the world) for new ways to do things when operations are no longer rolling smoothly. They look outside their current processes, beyond the traditional playbook, and turn on a dime to implement the better way.

Disruptors are willing to implement or adapt solutions used in completely unrelated fields and even foreign countries. Maybe it's an efficiency model used in aerospace applied to a restaurant's kitchen or an approach to employee engagement borrowed from a tech startup on the other side of the globe. The common thread? Curiosity. Disruptors are always asking, "What's the best way?" When their business isn't thriving, they don't settle—they adapt, innovate, and keep moving forward.

Disrupt to Thrive

Being a disruptor might be a way to save your business. Maybe not. But disrupting never means you must abandon everything you've built and start over. It means being willing to change, adapt, and grow. It's about looking beyond what's comfortable and pushing the boundaries of what's possible. When you start by disrupting your internal processes, always use your internal customers to their maximum potential and keep your eye on meeting and exceeding your external customers' needs and expectations—every good outcome is possible.

It's the people you develop who make everything happen. *Everything.* I need to pound on this point yet again:

So many businesses miss the mark on developing their internal customer service. Don't be that business. Don't forget your internal customers are (human) resources. Use your resources! You cannot expect to disrupt the marketplace if your internal processes are stuck in the same old routine, and your people are never called on for their ideas and never authorized to initiate solutions for clients. Start by letting innovation flow within your entire team and notice how it ripples outward ... and down to an increased bottom line.

What Sets Disruptors Apart?

To become a disruptor in your field, you need to ask and answer hard questions:

- "What makes us different from everyone else and is that good or bad?"

- "What don't our customers like about us or about our direct competitors? How do we fix that?"

- "What are we doing that is unique, and where are we just following the crowd?"

- "How can we offer something no one else is offering—or offer it in a way no one else is delivering ... and be meeting or exceeding customer expectations?"

Your goal is to reshape for the better how your external customers perceive what you do, why you do it, and how you do it. Disruption doesn't happen by accident. As when analyzing mistakes and successes, you engage your whole team which must now analyze your internal processes, and brainstorm their solutions to make their work easier, faster, smarter, and repeatable. You encourage everyone to "borrow inspiration" by looking at what's working in completely different industries both at home and in other countries. Above all, you make it safe for your team to challenge the norms. Identify the legacy "rules" of your industry—which might only be traditions and not rules at all. The most successful disruptors often break the rules that surprise and delight their customers, not to mention their staff. Finally, everyone comes together to test and try out the innovation. Not every idea will be a fit, and you won't be sure unless you are open to learning and to refine your approach to finding what works.

Internal Customer Disruption

All that said, to be a disruptor, the first thing to do as leaders or as internal customers is to get uncomfortable. Today's leaders might be lost when it comes to technology and (we are seeing this a lot!) don't understand the concept of AI, so use your tech-curious younger staff to stay on top of technology or report to the team on the latest trends so you can stay ahead of the curve. Other industry leaders might be uncomfortable about changing production methods, but again, you go out on the factory floor and get the internal customers closest to the production process involved. Stretch yourselves!

Being disruptive means taking an action no one in your sector has ever taken, either internally or externally. Until you know what the trends are, you can't buck the trend. Until you know how/if any solution might benefit your business, you have to test, try, and try again.

I admit I am not one of those tech-savvy leaders, but I keep my ear to the ground. I learned how to use our current tools by being a customer of other businesses.

- Maybe no one in your sector is sending video emails to educate consumers. *Loom* allows you to share AI-powered videos with transcriptions in a sidebar window and embed the whole message in an email (Loom.com).

- Maybe you have international customers, but emailing isn't good enough. *Synthesia* (Synthesia.io) turns your texts into videos, with a choice of 140 languages.

- Maybe your old tools have made you sluggish in your marketing and lead generation. *Content Captain* (ContentCaptain.io) automates and optimizes your content strategy and lead generation processes.

Of course, by the time you read this, those tools may have been surpassed and replaced, but the idea is that there is probably someone on your staff complaining right now about not having an AI tool to perform XYZ task in your business. So? Give the technically curious of all ages an official company challenge to identify and test the top ten AI (or whatever your team sees as worth exploring) tools out there that satisfy the needs of that task. Give them a small budget and time frame to do this. Let your employees be creative. Then have them make a short pitch about the tools they found and why they would or wouldn't be great in your business. This is good when you actually need some new automations or upgrades to tools you're using now—and allows you to be that disruptor. Never fail to honor the employee who identifies the one the company ends up buying and installing.

Take Risks

To be a disruptor, you have to take a risk and that means some initial discomfort. This disruptive discomfort applies even to areas I would not particularly call "disruptive" but are simply new to the leader or business. I have a nonprofit client who is always fundraising. I introduced them to a professional to apply for a tax credit that would have been advantageous for them. Although others have confirmed getting a million dollars back in tax credits by doing this, my nonprofit client was too afraid to even look at it. The organization lost out on quite a bit of tax credit money even though it would've helped their cause and their organization immensely. (Was the issue that old fear of the IRS? I never could find out what caused their resistance.)

Go Off-Script

To be a disruptor, you may have to go off the industry script. That script is just a set of traditions—ways "every business in your industry" does things. You might need to take up a different business model. A free lunch once a month or a Christmas party is no longer what today's employees are looking for from their employers—that's "so twentieth century!" Step up your game.

Benefits are one of those industry scripts. The type and number of benefits you offer are one of the reasons employees choose to work for you, like it or not. How to innovate? Your internal customers should be the ones leading the way here.

Ask your employees what types of benefits they actually want. Disrupt the pattern of the standard benefits packages. Custom employee benefits can distinguish you as word gets out in the marketplace that you're doing something different or better. Your goal is to offer a different, more relevant menu of options, not just the standard ones everyone else is unilaterally offering their employees. Aflac grabbed this unmet need and disrupted the field of employee benefits and insurance coverage. It came to businesses with a long menu of specific, individually priced, supplemental insurance coverage options that their staff could choose to fit their needs. From childcare accounts to specific cancer care, their coverages were popular because their external customers could make them relevant to their needs.

Who uses this employee-driven benefits packaging? Disruptors do. Transformational leaders do.

Revisit Legacy Business Practices

Companies that have been in business for a while need to review what and how they're doing things—a refresh and reset. Get all your employees together to determine the relevance of every aspect of the business as an ongoing exercise uniting all your internal customers.

Maybe some procedures or tools you use remain relevant because of your niche, but then, how can you improve, expand, clarify, renew, or modernize them? Don't stick with your ten-year-old startup choices—or your hundred-year-old way of doing a thing—just because you are risk-averse. You *want* to disrupt what you're doing, and internal customers will be enthusiastic about participating in the disruption. Look at it as one aspect of your continuous operations improvement.

A disruptor is continuously reviewing processes, procedures, tools, training, messaging, branding effectiveness, and so on—all designed to beat the competition and to gain more customers. And speaking of training...

Offer Education

Educational offers are another disruptor tool. They come in many forms in US businesses. Paid time off to pursue an MBA or a GED. Company-paid tuition in full or some other amount. These offers are directly or indirectly related to the work you do. The benefit is that the company pays and, as much as possible, offers the education on company time.

Offer benefits education. If you offer a retirement savings program such as a 401(k), don't assume your non-financial internal customers know anything about taxes, tax deferral, investing, vesting, or any of the rest. Bring in an outside trainer to do an educational workshop on company time. Employees will tell you they're much more comfortable saving money now that they have more knowledge. They'll start to max out their accounts because they know what that means to them.

Offer skills-related education resulting in a certification in a trade or a software application. Have annual refresher training for advanced users of the software tools everyone relies on to be sure all staff use it properly and fully. Initial training is not even done in many businesses. Be the disruptor. Efficiency will expand.

There are more possibilities, of course, but your internal customers will see you offering education *relevant to them and not just your business needs*. It increases loyalty. It increases their buy-in to your company. It develops confidence, skills, and engagement. Your employees then go out and tell their friends what a great company they work for, and you become one of the companies that people want to work for.

External Customer Disruption

Those were just some examples of how you can beneficially disrupt and step up your internal customer service. How are you refreshing what you're offering to external customers?

Remember drive-in theaters with speakers that clipped to your car window? In my area in Massachusetts, we have one of those. It was just sitting there, more or less abandoned until a well-known local food business purchased it. They offer *Food and Fun* there now. The drive-in is now a foodie destination with a beer garden. And, yes, it's still a drive-in. They repositioned this old drive-in as a daytime-nighttime destination. They disrupted the whole view of drive-in theaters in people's minds—and in the process created a new destination that had been lacking in the region.

If you're in the insurance business, how do you disrupt? Think about why people make claims on their homeowner's insurance: because something went wrong. Why not offer a booklet referring to local flooring, plumbing, electrical, furniture and home decor, lawn care, and other businesses? Those businesses pay you, the insurance business, to list them in the booklet. Who does that? A disruptor does. Sure, the client still makes a claim; but you've saved them and you time with proactive solutions.

Refresh your delivery models. During COVID, restaurants had to—or die. They built drive-through windows and added delivery services where that hadn't been their model before. Yes, the public knew those models, but it was only the proactive businesses who retained their loyal customers throughout the pandemic.

Service businesses like attorneys, physicians, and consultants previously worked only face-to-face with clients in their own offices. COVID pushed that disruption, too, and now it's almost the norm to have a Zoom medical consultation or to chat on a web conference with your attorney.

Disrupt by need but also disrupt by choice when it enhances your external customer experience.

My business, HPS, is in professional development. That also used to be a face-to-face business. However, we've looked at AI and AI avatars, virtual reality, videos embedded with URL links, and really anything that's intuitive and immediately useful to our clients. We're constantly looking to refresh our approaches.

All for the Wow

We all realize that software, smartphone manufacturers, and all sorts of other tech businesses are putting new products out every six months. They're telling the marketplace to keep up because they're coming out with a brand-new wow for us.

You must wow, too, whatever your activity.

Do an inventory to see what's working and what's not, both internally and externally, with enhanced external customer experience in mind. Do a serious analysis of the marketplace—and do it every six months. Use the findings to determine how you can do better than others.

The disruptor is a business that flips the script in order to "wow." Apple disrupted the telephone market. They put legacy telecom companies built around corded and cordless landline phones in the hot seat and nearly out of business. Sears & Roebuck was a brick-and-mortar store that broke the mold way back when with their "Wish Books"—their thick mail-order catalogs. Customers who were hundreds of miles from any Sears store could phone or write in their order for anything in the catalog, and it would be delivered to their door. Wow (and back then, it was—ask great-grandma).

Amazon, our mega-mail-order business, took that model further with the advent of the internet. It was a wow disruptor and is now putting shopping malls out of business. The gamble has paid off: Amazon sales accounted for an estimated 37.6 percent of US e-commerce spending in 2023, and some analysts say it's closer to 50 percent.[25]

This is disruption! This is the big wow! The disruptors first flipped the script, and did it by bringing consumers that new wow, that new, bright and shiny must-have product. What's the next big "wow" in your industry? The next "wow"

---

25 Seamus Breslin, "20 Amazon Statistics You Need to Know in 2024," Repricer Express, January 29, 2024, https://www.repricerexpress.com/amazon-statistics. For the curious among you, Amazon's net revenue increased by over $40 billion year-on-year, from $513.98 billion in 2022 to $554.02 billion in 2023.

for your internal customers? How will that energy translate into wowing your clients not just once, but consistently, time and time again?

Consider how industries like healthcare and law have embraced personalization and left their legacy operations in the dust. Pre-COVID, the idea of doctors or attorneys hopping on a Zoom call with patients or clients was unthinkable. But now? It's standard practice, and it's a game-changer. The willingness to adapt and to meet external customers where they are demonstrates that the relationship is important to you. It builds trust and creates loyalty.

Customer Loyalty and Staff Retention

A lot of innovation is just building on or redirecting what already exists. Yes, much of this disruption to the ways we do things is imposed by outside circumstances. But a competitor is also an outside circumstance, wouldn't you say? Your competitors, if you're honest, steal both your external and internal customers, and it may just be because they're innovating, disrupting, and *beating you at your own game.*

Jim Collins is the author of the continuously #1-ranked business book on Amazon entitled *From Good to Great.*[26] Let me point out how hard it is to reach and remain number one in Amazon's bookstore—that's how great this book is and why you need your own copy. It is also an example whose concepts don't get old no matter how many years go by.

---

26 Jim Collins, *Good to Great: Why Some Companies Make the Leap . . . and Others Don't* (Harper Business, 2001).

The premise? *Good is the enemy of great. Fine is the enemy of outstanding. Okay is the enemy of stellar.* There are a lot of "good enough" companies and "good enough" products and services out there. "Average" is the majority of businesses, almost by definition. Disrupt. Be great.

I know of a twenty-two-year-old man who decided to start a valet company—a parking service such as we see offered by some restaurants, stores, hotels, and others. He disrupted straight out of the gate on day one. He taught his staff to be sure they're opening doors for drivers and passengers getting out of and into the vehicles. They offer to get gas for the client if they're low on gas and do so while the client is doing whatever they came to do. Clients can text when they're on their way back to the car so that it's ready and warmed up or cooled down according to the weather. His valets are in uniform—easily identifiable to customers. The business sends notes after a company or individual uses them. Staff are employees, not contractors, and they work full-time, so they get all kinds of benefits.

Contrast that approach to any legacy company out there where the service is "fine," the food (or other product/service) is "fine," the price is "okay"... but the business owners have never tried to move that perception from fine to great. It should be clear by now to you why that's so. They have not disrupted.

Call it disruption, call it innovation, call it brainstorming with internal customers at every mistake and every success. Whatever you call it, it starts with your employees.

They're the ones who will follow processes and procedures that serve the external client and build that loyalty. They're the ones that shrink your costs, drive your profits, and take your business to the next level.

That's why recruiting the right people is so crucial. How and who you hire suddenly takes on a whole new level of importance. Retaining those employees is what truly fuels growth and innovation. High turnover keeps your team stuck in the basics, constantly onboarding and retraining rather than innovating, disrupting, and building momentum. On the other hand, a team that stays with you becomes a well-oiled machine—if, and only if they're given the tools and opportunities to grow.

What Long-Term Employees Bring to the Table

A team that sticks around isn't just experienced—they're invested. They've built trust, streamlined your processes, and become the backbone of your business, not to mention knowing your products inside out. They feel ownership of all that because you've called upon them time and again to improve upon it! To keep that talent and energy in-house, you need to create an environment that excites and empowers them. Here's what that looks like:

- **Empowerment through tools:** Employees thrive when they have access to state-of-the-art, disruptive tools, equipment, and processes that make their work more efficient and impactful.

Professional training on using those tools skyrockets their effectiveness.

- **Excitement to adapt and get ahead of the pack:** Employees who have stayed aren't resistant to change—they're eager for it when it's presented as an opportunity for growth. Excite them with chances to disrupt, innovate, and implement. Then watch how quickly they adapt and thrive.

- **Clarity of purpose:** Everyone wants to feel like they're part of a big success story. When you clearly communicate how their role contributes to the company's overall success, they become more involved and more likely to stick around.

When you hear about companies with a fair number of twenty- or thirty-year employees, there's always a reason why they have stayed. It's not because those businesses were the only option in town. It's because those employers did right by their internal customers. They listened, they invested in their employees' development, and they empowered their people to not only make mistakes but also learn from them. They solicited their staff's input and acted on it.

Internal customer retention isn't an accident any more than long-term external customer loyalty is. It's the result of deliberate efforts to build a workplace where employees feel their skills and contributions are purposefully utilized, and where they are questioned and heard. They are provided with the resources and support needed. Retention happens in a workplace whose leaders tell them in many ways "You are capable of achieving your best" so that is what they provide. When you achieve that, your team doesn't just stay—they become advocates and promoters for your business because they are proud to say, "I'm part of this company."

Differentiating Yourself Through Disruption

At the end of the day, disruption and innovation are about doing the unexpected, pushing boundaries, asking "Why?" and "Who wrote that rule?", and finding new ways to deliver extraordinary value to internal and external customers alike. Your staff is counting on your business to thrive. Your customers are counting on you to deliver a product or service they need, want, and want to buy again and again.

By focusing on your internal customers and what they need and want and know, you set the stage for growth and differentiation that leaves your competitors in the dust and wondering what hit them.

As a disruptor bringing great value to your internal and external customers, you must hire today with the future in mind. You must have a program whose goal is to retain your best talent and help them grow. You must enable your team, through unfettered creativity and permission, to innovate and adapt to disruption in your industry.

People Profit

Attracting and keeping talent is not all about money. Managers and other leaders assume, with a wave of the hand, that it's always wages and salaries that lead employees to quit a job—all the while understanding that's far too simplistic a reason.

Once you've correctly hired, trained, and continued to develop your internal customers, you need to keep disrupting, innovating, improving, and *listening* to retain them.

Here is Gartner's summary of what drives employees to quit, and I encourage you to examine the reasons and think about how you can flip that script and increase your business's staff retention time.

Employees quit because . . .

1. **Something is broken:** The company doesn't recognize their contributions; there are no opportunities for growth and the company is not investing in them; the manager doesn't further their career.

2. **Competing employers are doing better:** There are more interesting companies out there where they could develop and deploy their skills better. Other companies will pay them 20 percent more for the same work.

3. **Needs are not being met:** They are not only burning out, but your company also doesn't align with their social values. They have no flexibility in your job and their lifestyle is way off what they need and want. They want to go back to school, and your business doesn't offer that flexibility. [27]

---

[27] Chart from Gartner Insights/Human Resources/Article: "Great Resignation or Not, Money Won't Fix All Your Talent Problems" December 9, 2021 Contributor: Jackie Wiles https://www.gartner.com/en/articles/great-resignation-or-not-money-won-t-fix-all-your-talent-problems Accessed January 4, 2025

Conclusion

The motivation someone has for founding and leading a business varies depending on who you ask. Some leaders are product-focused, driven by the dream of getting their innovation out into the world. Others are service-minded, eager to provide solutions that make life better for their customers. And, of course, there are those who are in it for financial freedom, whether it's personal wealth, time flexibility, or delivering impressive returns for investors and shareholders.

However, no matter the motivation—whether you're managing a team with a narrow function vital to the business, running the company with a far and clear horizon in sight, or steering a global enterprise—it all comes down to one undeniable core truth: Businesses are about people. Say "people" and you really mean "relationships."

It's not just about the products you sell, the services you provide, or the numbers on the balance sheet. Your business thrives because of the people behind the scenes who make it happen and the customers who trust you enough to choose what you offer. The sooner leaders recognize this, the stronger their businesses and their legacies become.

The Heart of Your Business

Your product wouldn't reach the market without the talented people who produce it, market it, sell it, and maintain or upgrade it along the way. It's always going to be your people who bring your business to life.

As leaders, it's important to remember that every dollar earned, every milestone achieved, and every success celebrated comes from the collective effort of your people. They are the resources that make the magic happen, and they're the heart and soul of everything your business accomplishes.

When you invest in, value, and empower your staff, you're not just supporting the people behind the scenes. You're strengthening the foundation and (internal and external) reputation of your entire business. To truly thrive, it's essential to understand who your customers are, what they value, and how to connect with them in meaningful ways. Business is, and always will be, about relationships—the ones you build with your customers and the ones they build with your brand.

Conclusion

When you prioritize those connections, you're not just selling a product or service. You're creating trust, loyalty, and a community of people who believe in what you do.

Business is all about the relationships.

Throughout these pages, we've explored the relationships that form the backbone of every business—what I've called internal and external customer service. These relationships are the driving force behind your success. Your business can't thrive in the long term, operate at peak efficiency, or achieve a profit that benefits everyone unless you invest in both groups and cultivate those connections with care.

At the very start of this book, I pointed out the customer service gap I've observed in so many businesses—that space between what companies deliver and what clients expect and hope for. The entrepreneur and people-person in me can't help but wonder how much more successful these businesses could be if they bridged that gap. Are they leaving predictable, sustainable growth on the table simply because they're not prioritizing these crucial relationships?

As you move forward, I challenge you to remember this: Your people—both internal and external—are the true source of your profit. Nurture your employees and your clients with intention and care. Use the strategies we've explored in these pages and implement them in ways that resonate with your unique team and culture. When you do, you're not just building a business—you're creating something extraordinary: a workplace where people feel valued, a brand your customers trust, and a legacy of success that lasts far beyond today.

About the Author

Sandra Coker is the visionary CEO of Human Power Solutions, a premier leadership and development consulting firm based in Westborough, Massachusetts. With over two decades of experience in organizational development, talent management, and strategic leadership, Sandra has dedicated her career to helping companies build resilient, high-performing teams. Through her company, she offers customized training programs that focus on leadership development, employee engagement, and organizational efficiency.

Sandra's expertise spans multiple industries, and she has worked closely with executives, managers, and emerging leaders whose goal is to foster a culture of continuous learning and growth that leads to higher employee involvement and retention as well as to improved top-line and bottom-line business outcomes. Her innovative approach combines practical strategies with an emphasis on human connection, which makes her a sought-after facilitator and speaker. Sandra's passion in writing this book is to provide actionable insights for leaders who are striving to empower their teams and to navigate today's evolving workplace challenges for greater profitability.

Sandra holds a Master of Science in Organizational Leadership (MSOL). She is the mother of three adult children, the grandmother of two grandchildren, and an avid motorcyclist who loves all outdoor activities.

Learn more about Human Power Solutions or book an exploratory conversation with Sandra at HPowerSolutions.com.

Made in the USA
Middletown, DE
10 March 2025